SECRETS
TO
SUCCESS
IN THE
CORPORATE WORLD

1st Printing 2011

PROFESSIONAL
SPEAKERS
ASSOCIATION
OF SOUTHERN AFRICA

Publisher:
Professional Speakers Association of Southern Africa (PSASA)
www.psasouthernafrica.co.za

Layout, drawings & cover design: Wolfgang Riebe

Copyright © 2011 by PSASA
www.psasouthernafrica.co.za

ISBN: 1453893156

EAN-13: 9781453893159

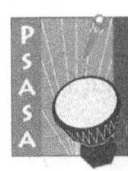

CONTENTS

Foreword... 4

Who put you in a box?
    Annie Coetzee.. 5

Stop sabotaging your dreams...
    Claire Newton... 20

Answering the call
    Eddie Botes.. 37

Grow your business
    Ian Rheeder.. 49

Edge of rain
    Jacques De Villiers.................................... 67

A safety perspective
    Jürgen Tietz... 80

The simple success system
    Richard Mulvey... 97

How can you thrive?
    Sharon King... 114

Balance your life
    Wilhelm Lombard...................................... 133

Passion is success
    Dr Wolfgang Riebe...................................148

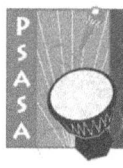

FOREWORD

Message from Dr Wolfgang Riebe.
2010/11 National President of the PSASA.

One of my goals in my term of national presidency was to put the PSASA on the map and to create an awareness within the corporate industry of the many talented professional speakers we have in our association.

Hence this first book of our new regular series of books with tips and advice from our speakers. You will not only get to know, but learn from many of our industry experts.

What comes across very strongly is that there is a similar thread in all the contributions, even though they have all been written by different speakers.

Without further ado, enjoy Secrets to Success in Corporate Life.

Warmest Wishes
Wolfgang

WHO PUT YOU IN A BOX?

ANNIE COETZEE

Annie Coetzee is an internationally recognised speaker, author and trainer on human empowerment, with 12 years of extensive experience in the corporate environment. In 2008, her seventh book "Are you connected?" was launched and proved to be the first book on human empowerment that places the HEART as central to human development. Annie is a regular keynote presenter during women empowerment conferences.

Annie has developed the first of over 40 wellness and longevity programs in SA that includes all 11 intelligences, and also wrote the first book in SA on 'Emotional Intelligence'. As one of the trendsetters in SA on the "Mind-and-Body-Connection" with strong emphasis on the heart, she has been invited to conduct exclusive 'in-house' seminars to help managers create the chemistry for PEAK performance in the corporate environment.

Annie left her position as a lecturer in Psychology at the University of Stellenbosch in the late eighties to live her passion as a fulltime researcher, author and speaker. She is currently the Pretoria Chapter President of the Professional Speakers Association of SA and also the editor of their national newsletter.

> Tel: (012) 346 0284
> Cell: 083 270 1995
> annie.coetzee@mweb.co.za
> www.anniecoetzee.co.za

WHO PUT YOU IN A BOX?

Don't be misled by the simplicity of this title.
Millions of people live lives that are not true to who and what they honestly are. Millions more also don't see, dream, speak and live the way they want to. These many millions have become what OTHERS believe or say about them.

Have you ever been told by someone that you are a 'typical TYPE A personality'? Or has any colleague of yours suggested that you should express more enthusiasm at work because that might make you look more interested in the project you're working on? And all this, while you are happily and sincerely interested in the project, but simply didn't show it the way the 'other' person expected you to show it!

Has it happened to you where a person in any group where you worked left a remark like, "Perhaps you should change your approach to the situation, you appear to be distant and disloyal to our clients."
Well, maybe similar remarks have been made about you – and deep inside you, you felt betrayed or hurt, because in your heart you know that you were true to yourself and do express your thinking in an authentic way.

I've heard the strangest things. One of them was, "You sleep too much – sleeping is a waste of time." Now imagine it was said to you and you are a happy, fun-filled and creative person, who does sleep more than the one who said it to you!
Are you now going to sleep less?
And what may the outcome of this decision be?

Perhaps your story is different.

Maybe an uncle or colleague has said to you, "It's normal to have backache after a long day's work." And maybe you have never questioned this opinion! Chances are you never felt comfortable about the remark either. But you heard it and somehow started acting as if this person's words were true. There might be days that you are 'waiting' for the backache to start!

The title: "WHO put you in a box?" is certainly most definitely a **self-empowerment** subject and leads to full-blast success. If we try to explain 'self-empowerment' in more ways, we can use words like splendid, opulent, magnificent, luminous, inspiring, blessed and healthy. We can also think in terms of stretching in a forward direction, while being renewed, surprised, uplifted and energised.

Therefore, zooming into this life-changing title, it will make sense if I share with you my thoughts on Conquering NORMAL.

The word 'normal' has a variety of meanings to different people. Some say it's normal to feel lazy on a Sunday afternoon, or it's normal to feel anxious before an interview with your new employer, or it's normal to gain weight when you are over fifty. Others expect to have pain and fatigue after a hard day's work. It's not really THAT dangerous to think 'normal' – but read on – being 'normal' holds many possibilities to put you in a box.

Einstein said, "Common sense is the collection of prejudices acquired at the age of eighteen". Through our life's experiences, we have all come up with so-called answers of what to expect from life. We sometimes refer to this as common sense. We look back at our memories and we establish and accept what we think is normal or common, and this becomes many peoples' expectation for life.

Even right now, as I'm sitting here and type, I can hear the voices of people I personally know, saying "What has been – will always be. Life has its patterns, and who are you to change that?"

Believe me, I have learned to block off the energy and vibrations coming towards me that try to stifle my creativity and constructive flow. It's important to know about this. It matters in life and business. It matters to what degree we are aware of what 'others' think 'normal' is for us!

In ancient times there was a common practice called 'assimilation.' When one nation conquered another nation, they assimilated the people into their own culture. The rulers were very clever. They knew that it was the difference in CULTURE that caused mistrust and uncertainty. These rulers used power and often other creative strategies to 'pull the newcomers into their camps' - knowing that if they do not eradicate the people's former ways of thinking, it may lead to separation and even wars. So they assimilated them into 'being one' with them.

Another way of looking at this, is to think of these historical happenings, as what was 'being normal'. I'll try and explain this in a modern way: If your children emigrate to another country (mine did), and they want to become part of the new country's ways of living, they have to accept what is 'normal' in that country. They have to become part of the CULTURE of that country: Do what they do, shop like they shop, let the children participate in the same sports events, attend functions that might help them to blend in with the new countries' habits. If they don't, they might never feel a sense of belonging and who knows, never be happy!

Looking at this, there isn't really anything wrong with that, but allow me to go deeper.

CULTURE, or 'being normal' is established when people reach the limits to which they are willing to live. Then, to justify their position, they create groups (or paradigms) in an attempt to use the power of numbers to feel comfortable with the limitations they have accepted. In several circles, it is referred to as a 'party spirit'.

Question: Think of any example in your own life where you have felt 'left out' because of what the 'norm' of a certain situation was, even if you didn't feel to do what 'others' believe was right.

Here is the possible danger of 'normal': Once we begin to accept what 'normal' is, we limit ourselves. Being 'normal' limits our capacity to experience new breakthroughs, or go beyond established patterns and do things that are ahead of that limitation. It can without a doubt also inhibit your creativity and uniqueness.

The good news is that there is often that ONE person who breaks what 'normal' is in many situations. Take your mind back to when the first mile was run in less than four minutes. Once a person breaks a certain 'record' it isn't long before that record becomes the new 'normal'!

Isn't it time we break through some of the limitations that have been placed in our culture or environment and conquer the 'normal opinions' about matters – whether these relate to business, health, personal relationships or anything else affecting your life in a negative way!

Question: What is YOUR definition of what is 'normal' when you try to define 'success' in business?

Could it be something like, "Successful people pay a huge price – they usually end up either ill or divorced".

Think deep: You have to choose your own reality and create your own 'normal' about what success means to you.

"Who put you in a box?" is also a subject that strongly relates to **human energy.** Everything in the world is made out of molecules and this means energy: you, me, your keyboard, the table, your telephone, the grass and plants in your garden! To put it straight: absolutely everything! And since energy is vibration, it means that everything that exists - vibrates.

Question: What are you vibrating?

Has someone in your immediate presence recently told you that you come across as 'irritated'. That might be just another way of telling you what you are vibrating. (Of course, this person might also have told you something positive and exciting! I only want to make you think.)

Whether we can see it or not, **energy is pure, pulsing, ever-flowing movements and it's always moving towards something.** The inherent character of energy is to flow towards a manifestation of some sort. Modern day physicists and scientists agree that energy and matter are one and the same. However, they vibrate differently. Picture any musical instrument in your mind.

The sound that flows out from a violin is different than that from an organ, whose sound and energy flow is deeper and lower. The sounds, which are movement and energy, touch us. We respond. We feel something.

Unlike the tones from a musical instrument, the energy that flows out from you and me comes from our magnificently and highly developed brain, heart and complete body:

Crazy as that may sound, it's high time we woke up to the fact that we are all electro-magnetic-beings, moving in wonderfully, electrifying bodies, running around with this all-encompassing capacity to influence and be influenced by others.

Face it: we are all influenced by what others say about us and what they think about us, even though we often act as if "words don't hurt" or "words can't break us". Think again!

When a person is going through a stage of not feeling good, they send out low-frequency vibrations. Low frequency vibrations are every bit as powerful as high frequencies and they will attract unpleasant stuff back to you.

Sure as can be.
Because we live in a world with predominantly low frequency fields of energy, and billions of people who are vibrating more stress and anxiety than you might want to know of, we involuntarily absorb these vibrations and react to them. Especially when we are not vibrating our own high levels of energy.

I have learned to nurture my own and guard it against negative energy, as far as it is possible!

Verified research on **human energy** is fascinating.
Energy is and will always be part of us, wherever we go.

Energy! Energy! Energy!

It moves. It has to move. It is part of the nature of what energy is: It HAS to move and it moves because it has to create.

Do a small and simple test about the above: Stay in the presence of an angry, resentful and negative person for a while.

See how long and to what degree it affects you.

And then – accept the fact that you have to get rid of the energy if you find yourself struggling with constructive and creative tasks.
Here are some suggestions:

- Stop doing what you are busy with and do sit-ups, push-ups and/or any other kind of indoor activity for a few minutes. While you're doing this, visualise how the negative energy surrounding you, is leaving you. It's not difficult, it simply asks for childlike imagination and physical action;

- Once again, stop doing what you are busy with and listen to music. (CD, MP3, I-pod) As you are listening to the music, actively take your focus off your current moment and project yourself into a quiet space where you are free of the negative energy. Mental pictures are part of creative imaging techniques and are very beneficial.

The point is that you have to **consciously be aware** of the fact that the negative energy in your personal space **can** leave you, if you let it!

You might find more creative ideas to get rid of negative energy.

The journey of success is full of discoveries and you should be willing to go off the 'beaten track' and try 'different ways' to get to your destination.

I now want you to think about the meaning and consequences of what it means to be "**boxed in**".

Well, to start with, **it's NOT pleasant** and very uncomfortable!

However – get passionately involved in this journey of empowerment and breaking out of the box, or more than one. You will embrace the experience once you start sensing the truth about living in a box!

What I find most regretful is the fact that many times the box you are sitting in, is created and designed by someone else – someone who **thinks** he or she knows more about you than you know about yourself.

It can be a previous school teacher who said that "you're really slow when it comes to mathematical issues" and you have never forgotten these words.
It may also be that every time you work with figures, your brain slows down and you find yourself in a space of unhappy places. You've been put in a box!
When we were children, we never washed our hands with 'detergents' so that we could be free of infections and not get bacteria to 'crawl' on our skins…! We played in the sand, we hurt ourselves, we got into a bath and whoever washed or bathed us, used any soap available!

I was one of six children, our neighbours around my dad's farm also had big families – and I cannot recall one incident where any of us got infections because the soap we used didn't protect us from bacteria.

TODAY, with all the marketing around 'using the RIGHT soap' to fight infections and bacteria, it has become 'normal' to buy these products for our children or grandchildren and someone out there has become very wealthy.

The point I am making may be irrelevant for business success – it may help to make you **think** who is influencing you and to what degree, and if you benefit by that.

Too often we read or hear something, and without consciously deciding what to 'let go' and what to take in and consider, we start to believe what these people say and we "get into a box".

The **real you** might have been affected by these opinions. The real you might have been fatigued, vulnerable or ill when you heard these words, and your energy waves found 'matching vibrations' and you got into a box!

I've read somewhere: **"Spaces define, confine and divide."**

Being put in a box, or simply getting into a box, does the same to people. This or that box defines you, another box confines you, and being in different boxes divides you. In actual fact, it means that you become different persons, to fit every box, to be accepted by what someone has said - or wants you to be.

Stressful – to say the least.

Instead of being one, constant, well-balanced and creative force of energy, you are more like a whole bunch of energy bundles, each having a different frequency, ready to move all over the place with up-down, up-down vibrations, to fit every situation.

Can you imagine the negative energy flowing between these boxes? I personally think 'boxes' are some of the most important reasons why there are so many relationship breakdowns in our world:

> *People use boxes to store things in.*
> *Or keep secrets inside them.*
> *Or put something away and out of sight.*

This is scary. But don't worry. There are ways to get out!

It is often not only words that put people in a box.

It can be someone else's thinking about you.
It can also be someone's feelings about you.

These are all part of the ENERGY messages I'm sharing with you in this book.

The following sections in this chapter contain examples of situations to illustrate how easy it can be to get into a box:

1. A while ago your dance partner has said that you have 'feet like an elephant' when you dance. In your head, you have never forgotten these words, and also never released them from your memory. You want to dance more, but every time you think about an exciting dance event and want to go, your feet feel heavy and daft. You just don't go.

2. Your husband is a good golfer. You also started to play and find it hard and utterly frustrating. But you are willing to learn and willing to practice. Sadly, he keeps reminding you that 'it takes YEARS to perfect one's swing' and 'don't even THINK you can get a low handicap within five years!' If you accept these words, you will get into a box that confirms every word your husband has said.

3. You remain working for a certain company because they are loyal to you. You know they don't value your creative abilities neither the vision you have for the company and yourself. You don't leave, even after you have presented a number of well-researched ideas to the management team. Fit in? No! Boxed in? YES. Your vision could create a better place for you to be in a more progressive company.

4. You don't try any aerobic exercise to stay fit and healthy because your brother told you that the family suffers from weak bones. He also told you that aerobic exercises are, after all, not good for your joints. You have allowed his opinion to become a reality for you and it put you in a box – you became a couch potato!

5. You are naturally a happy person and loves to show your enthusiasm when the situation calls for it. However, someone in the company recently said that your expressive ways do not fit into their corporate image. You stopped showing your feelings. You allowed someone else's opinion of what is 'correct' and 'normal' to affect your own energetic flow of happy feelings. Sadly, this company has just 'boxed' someone who vibrates life-enhancing energy and masses of creativity.

6. You have been married twice. You are now divorced and a contented single person who belongs to a social group and enjoy life. But then someone in the group (possibly an insecure woman) said that you are a flirt and you try to make up on what you have lost in life. So you stopped dating and even stopped seeing some of your new-found friends, because you don't trust them. You've allowed that one person's opinion to take you away from people who are like you: mortal beings, hoping for another chance.

Question: Ask yourself if you are in ANY 'box' because of someone's mindless, unplanned and reckless thoughts, words and feelings. Write it down in your journal. And read on.

The most fascinating part about 'being boxed in' is that the person who is in the box, finds it natural to defend him/herself. It is a form of protection. It's instinct. It's an inborn human desire to get OUT.

I hope I have raised your awareness of possible, subtle insinuations and suggestions that have made you a defensive specie – your entire life revolving around credos of 'This is the way...'

It's quite funny isn't it? It's also sad.
And it happens to millions of people, every single day.

To put a smile on your face, let's THINK...
Once you are in a 'box', the first question I will ask you is:

"How far can you see from there!?"

I've got GOOD news.
JACK gets out of the box!

Imagine any box in your cupboard. Most of them have lids and some of the lids are heavy. Others have clips or latches. The objects in the box, whether this is jewelry or letters or whatever, stay in the box until someone opens the box.

You and I are not objects.
We are human beings with a brain, and a heart, and a body so wonderfully created, it is breathtaking.
The astonishing power and energy we are born with, makes it possible for us to get OUT of the box!

Remember, when Jack got out of the box, he was smiling...
He was pushing forward with gusto...
He wowed his audience!

Jack needed someone to open the box.
You and I don't. It will help! But we don't!

We can use our minds and hearts, the energy in our magnificent bodies and just LEAP out.

Let's add the element of surprise to this leaping out of the box, and use our energies to turn lives around and live our dreams.

I once read a story about a weight lifter in the UK who could not break the world record of 500 pounds. No matter how hard he tried, no matter how close he came to successfully reaching his goal, he just could not do it. Everybody in the weight-lifting circuits said that it was an impossible goal for his body mass. However – his coach decided to put extra weight on his bar during training sessions, **but did not tell him that he was doing it.** The weight lifter was not aware of the fact that he was lifting more than the 500 pounds during his practice sessions.
Somehow, this coach got the idea that he was "NOT going to keep him behind because of general opinions and former records".

Guess what? He broke the record!

Being in a box can also be compared to being normal.

I am so inspired to write about this subject that I often imagine how I tap into that perfect feeling where my frequencies are higher than a kite, and my love for those in boxes, more powerful than the sun.

And then I know, there are people in the world who have the gift of helping others out of their boxes.
The weight lifting coach was one of them.
Here are some practical suggestions on how to get OUT of "boxes".

- Identify what you don't want in life and know your boundaries with people. If you notice someone you have to work with, remains negative, tell this person about 'boxes' and human energy and ask him or her to respect your understanding about it.

- Identify what you DO want in life and when possible, select your team players carefully. You ARE a human being and you WILL influence, and be influenced.
- Don't think that the world has to change before you can be successful. Create your OWN space of creative energy, loving energy and healing energy.
- Don't wait for the FEEL good energies before you turn them on. Turn them on, all day long. Make it a habit. Buzz for no other reason than to keep your own energy vibrations high and positive.
- Guard your heart and mind and be selective what thoughts and feelings you nurture.
- Think hard and smart before you 'take hands' in business.
- KNOW that you are created to be a problem solver. Know that you are not a victim or a product of the past. Believe that you can create new beginnings every day.
- Get actively involved in your own life. Do not expect other people to make you happy or successful. Step out. Step UP. Get noticed for your positive and creative energy. You WILL draw the 'right kind' of person into your space!
- Do not be a wimpy-wanter person. DO want big and bountiful. DO want health and fitness. DO want happiness and personal fulfillment.

And when you sense you are in ANY kind of 'box' get OUT and wow us please!
Don't waste energy on banging, whacking, pounding, hammering and pushing. Just JUMP! You were born with the ability to do so! Remain feisty and fearless.

And lastly: Empowerment is also about **empowering OTHERS** – and you cannot do this when you're living in a box.

STOP SABOTAGING YOUR DREAMS...

CLAIRE NEWTON

Claire Newton is a qualified psychologist, speaker, trainer and coach. She holds a Master's Degree in Psychology and a Higher Diploma in Education, as well as a Certificate in Career and Executive Coaching. She is a member of the Health Professions Council of South Africa, the Durban Practicing Psychologists Group, Toastmasters International and is President of the Durban Chapter of the Professional Speakers Association of South Africa.

As a psychologist, Claire runs a successful private practice, as well as consults to corporate companies. She offers a variety of psycho-educational interventions, such as trauma counselling, retrenchment counselling, grief and bereavement forums, HIV&AIDS presentations as well as self-esteem development. She runs her private practice from her home in Durban.

As a trainer, Claire's experience is in the field of inter-personal skills. She is contracted to companies and facilitates for them, as well as running her own courses. These include Basic and Advanced Counselling Skills, and Communication Skills courses, among others. Her passion in all of this is what she refers to as "Personal Growth Work" – that is, helping people to be authentic, find meaning, and live happier, more effective lives. She develops people's **YOU-Q**!

Tel: (031) 261 7466
Cell: 082 491 1136
claire@clairenewton.co.za
www.clairenewton.co.za

STOP SABOTAGING YOUR DREAMS... START LIVING THEM!

We all have dreams for ourselves and our lives, and as business people, we have dreams for our careers.

We usually associate dreams with something good. We talk about a wonderful experience as something that was "beyond our wildest dreams" or "more than we ever dreamed of". We describe an unexpected pleasure as "something we've only ever dreamed about," and talk about "the stuff that dreams are made of."

Dreams are happy. Dreams are good.

They are also very, very possible.

I believe you can *make* your dreams your reality:

> *Reality can destroy the dream;*
> *why shouldn't the dream destroy reality?*
> *(George Moore)*

We all know that if we want to live the life of our dreams we need to have a plan and set goals. Teachers, motivational speakers and coaches have been telling us this for years....but it isn't working! Very few people are actually living the life they thought they would. The life they dreamed they would.

Why?

Because we sabotage our plans. Unconsciously, of course, but very effectively all the same!

We commit this sabotage in three ways:

- **We don't believe in ourselves.**
- **We don't make a plan for our own dreams.**
- **We don't review our plan regularly, to keep up to date with the changes that are happening in our lives.**

These three factors are all interlinked, but in order to fully understand why we're not living our dream, we need to examine each one individually.

1. We Don't Believe In Ourselves

If we want to realise our dreams we *do* need to have a plan and set goals, but a plan on its own is not enough. We also need to have good self-esteem (self-esteem is the degree to which we value ourselves) because it is our *belief about ourselves* that *really* impacts on what we achieve in life.

If we have high self-esteem we value ourselves. We think good things about ourselves, we like ourselves and we think we are worthy and capable.

If we have low self-esteem we don't value ourselves. We don't like ourselves, and think we think we are useless, worthless and not good enough. We certainly don't think we are capable of achieving much.

The sad thing about self-esteem is that it is not necessarily based on truth or fact.

As a child, we learned to judge our worth based on what *other* people said or did to us – significant people like our parents, siblings, teachers and friends. It didn't matter whether what they said or did was conscious and direct, or unconscious and indirect, it still had an impact. If our ideas and opinions were listened to, we learnt that what we had to say was worthwhile. If we were ignored, or told we were silly, we learnt that our opinions were stupid or didn't count. If the significant people in our lives spent time with us, we learnt that we were lovable and nice to be around, but if they never had time for us, we learnt that we were not lovable or nice to be around.

The result is that we evaluated our worth based on how we were treated (or even how we *perceived* we were treated). Although these evaluations may not be valid, they have the power to affect everything in our lives, because we continue to believe the things we believed as a child, right into our adulthood. Our mind continues to judge us now as it did then.

We hear it in that little voice in our head. The one that talks to us, constantly saying things like "You shouldn't be doing this, you really aren't good enough, you are making a fool of yourself, this is not for you..."

The executive in the boardroom who learned as a child that his opinion didn't count, will find it hard to express his opinion, because the little voice in his head will be telling him to keep his mouth shut to avoid making a fool of himself. But the woman who grew up with love and recognition will not be shy to go up to new colleagues and make friends – she knows she is good company.

An even sadder thing about our self-esteem is that it is self-perpetuating – we only see or believe what we expect to see or believe about ourselves.

For example, if someone believes they are a good public speaker, they will readily accept the praise and acknowledgment they get for delivering a great presentation. And even if the presentation goes badly, and they get negative feedback, they will just write if off to an audience who didn't understand what they were trying to say, or to the audio visual equipment not being up to scratch. They just won't believe it is their own lack of ability.

On the other hand, if someone has low self-esteem, they will only see and believe those things that prove they are useless. They won't pay attention to the 20 wonderful evaluations giving star ratings, but they will take to heart the *one* evaluation with a criticism.

Our past shapes our beliefs about ourselves - what our strengths and weaknesses are, what we are capable or incapable of achieving, and what we should or ought to be doing or not doing. This is critically important because it is our beliefs and feelings that cause us to behave the way we do.

Most people think that how we behave and what we achieve is the result of what happens to us, our environment, or the situations we find ourselves in, but this is not true. It is *not* the event that causes our behaviour – it is our beliefs and feelings *about* the event that cause our behaviour.

For example, you may think, "if my wife cheats on me, I'll leave her" or "if my husband hits me, I'll leave him".

But you forget about your beliefs and emotions - and beliefs and emotions change everything.

If your husband hits you, you may decide NOT to leave. Because you love him, because you believe you won't find anyone better, because you believe you can't cope without him, because you believe you should stay together 'until death do us part'…. and so on.

Different individuals experience the same situations in different ways – there is no "*reality*". Our behaviour or response depends on our beliefs and feelings – on our perception.

For example, the rand/dollar exchange rate suddenly drops drastically. Instead of being R7.00 to $1.00 it is now R2.00 to $1.00. How would you react?

If you are a **holiday-maker** planning to go on holiday in the USA on a tight budget, you will know that this is a positive change for you and you will be delighted that you will have so much more spending money. You will quickly make your currency exchange so as not to lose out.

If you are an **expatriate** working in a foreign country and being paid in dollars, you will know this is a negative change for you and will be disappointed that you are not able to send so much money home to your family. You may start wondering if it is worth it to work so far away from home, for so little money.

If you are **retired** and living off your money invested in dollars in an offshore account, you will be devastated. You will cut back drastically on your monthly spending so as to manage on your fixed Dollar income each month.

Our behaviour depends on our beliefs and feelings – on our perception.

What you are capable of achieving depends on what you *believe* you can achieve:

> **"Whether you think you can,**
> **or whether you think you can't – you are right."**
> **(Henry Ford)**

So you need to become aware of what that little voice in your head is saying. Is it sabotaging you and telling you that you can't, or perhaps shouldn't, achieve your dreams?

Remember that:

> *"The most important judgement we will ever have to pass in life is the judgement we make on ourselves."*
> *(Source unknown)*

Stop the sabotage!

Review your set of beliefs about yourself and create new beliefs based on your current reality. You may need some help doing this, as our beliefs are mostly unconscious. (Even conscious beliefs are so much a part of us that we don't realise how they influence our behaviour). Have a few sessions with a psychologist to help you unpack your beliefs. Then create new beliefs that *do* allow you to achieve your goals.

It may be a good idea to write down a list of affirmations about yourself, and pin these somewhere where you can read them everyday. Keep adding to your list. An affirmation is a positive statement about yourself such as "I am organised and efficient", "I am fun to be around"," I am capable of making sound decisions". The idea behind reading these affirmations is that you replace the negative self talk you have been hearing in your head, with positive self talk because…

> *"Whatever your mind can conceive and believe,*
> *it can achieve."*
> *(Napoleon Hill)*

2. We don't make a plan for our own dreams

Do you want to get to the end of your life and realise that you have lived someone else's dream?

If the answer is no, then your plan needs to be about your dreams, because if you are not living **your** dream then you *are* living someone else's!

To do this, you need to become clear about what your dream is. Ask yourself important questions like:

What are my values?
What is my purpose?
What is my vision?
How am I going to get there?

It is important to know what your values are, because values give you direction. If you have to make an important decision in life, it is your values that will help you make that decision. Your values act as your compass, and you need to know where your true north is if you don't want to lose yourself as you travel the pathways of life.
Living a fulfilling versus an impoverished life has nothing to do with money – it has to do with achieving your goals according to your values.

Let me share a personal example.

I was offered a phenomenal job working for a company based in another city. The salary was fantastic, the perks even better, and I would have enjoyed the work in the main. My little eyes flashed dollar signs, just like in the cartoons, and I was extremely tempted, but at the same time I was ambivalent – I didn't want to work for someone else in an 'eight to five' job, and I didn't want to live in that city. Being confused and uncertain, I asked a few people for their opinion. Most said it was a great financial and career move - none understood what was most important for me. In the end it was my values that helped me to decide. I turned the job down as it wasn't right for me. It didn't fit my values of independence, change, variety and family. It would have given me lots of money, but that's not **my** true north.

Ask yourself: "What is true north for me?"

Here is a list of values. Which are the most important to you? Choose only five.

To do this, think about which of these you values you would compromise and which values you would never compromise.

Acknowledgement	Effectiveness	Integrity	Reliability
Adaptability	Energy	Intelligence	Sexuality
Beauty	Enthusiasm	Joy	Spirituality
Being admired	Excitement	Knowledge	Sport
Being alone	Expertise	Leadership	Stability
Being different	Fame	Love	Status
Being real / authentic	Family	Life balance	Success
Belonging	Fun	Money	Support
Change & variation	Freedom to choose	Nature	Time
Collaboration	Friendship	Order	Tradition
Communication	Helping others	Peace	Truth
Competition	Health	Personal growth	Wealth
Courage	Honesty	Popularity	Wisdom
Creativity	Humour	Power	
Commitment	Independence	Respect	

It is not as easy as you think to choose only five – it requires a lot of thought, and you need to be conscious of your inner voice and how it influences your choices.

Again, watch out for sabotage.

Ask yourself, "Are these really **my** values?" What is the little voice in your head saying? Whose voice is it really? Mom's? Dad's?

Stop the sabotage!
Choose your *own* values.

Put some time and effort into doing this - don't just accept that the values you were told to have as a child are **your** values. They may no longer be your values (and perhaps they never really were!)

Just as you must choose your own values, you must also choose your own purpose.

It is important to have a purpose because your purpose is the big picture of your life.
Most of us want to know what our purpose is in life.

Deepak Chopra said:

> *"The three big questions all people ask:*
> *Who am I?*
> *What do I want?*
> *What is my purpose?"*

Your purpose is the long-term reason why you are doing something. It gives meaning to your life. Your actions and goals are the short term means to achieving your purpose.

It is far more motivating to think about your purpose than your goals.

For example:

I am reading a book on presentation skills (action).
I want to develop myself into a speaker of international calibre (goal).
I want to make a positive impact on people all over the world, and help them to help themselves so they can live the life of their dreams right now (purpose).

Knowing my purpose motivates me to do the sometimes boring actions that I need to do.

Know what your purpose is. Spend time thinking about it. But watch out for sabotage:

When you think of your purpose, become conscious of what that little voice in your head is saying. Whose voice is it really? Ask yourself: "Is this really **my** purpose or has it been imposed on me by significant others?"

Stop the sabotage!
Create your *own* purpose.

When you know your own purpose you can create your own vision.

Vision is important, because if you don't know where you are going you won't get there:

> **"If a man knows not what harbour he seeks,
> any wind is the right wind."**
>
> **(Seneca)**

You need to know where you want to go. You *have* to know what your vision is – for yourself and your life.

To create your vision, think about your purpose and what you want to achieve with your life. Where would you like to see yourself in the future? What memories would you like to have when you look back on your life? What would you like other people to say about you and your life at your funeral? Think about all the different aspects of your life.

What inspires you?

It may be useful to create a vision board to help you clarify your vision. A vision board is a collection of pictures of things you want in life. Put this collection where you can see it. This focuses your unconscious mind, which in turn steers your choices toward making the vision real.

Beware – most people create the identical vision board... a mansion, a luxury car, a pile of cash, a good looking spouse, a gorgeous body and a tropical beach.

Boring! This is our culture's idea of the perfect life. Even a handsome millionaire, director of his own company, with a Ferrari in his garage and a mansion with a private beach will produce this sort of vision board. But is this *really* what *you* want?

To really work, your vision board must come not from society's impositions, but from your own deep and unique inner self.

Watch out for Sabotage. Ask yourself, "Am I living *my* life or somebody else's? Is this really my vision for myself? Become aware of what the little voice in your head is saying. Whose voice is it?"

Stop the sabotage!
Choose your *own* vision.

In creating your vision, there is just one tip I would like to give you:

Don't place too much emphasis on what time will destroy (body, looks etc), rather focus on that which time will enhance.

For example, don't go to gym to make yourself look like a twenty-something year old - you are fighting a losing battle. Go to gym to be fit, healthy and have energy – in this you can succeed.

Once you have got your vision you need to ask yourself: **How am I going to get there?**

The HOW is about the short-term steps that you need to take to achieve your final vision. It is not enough just to have a vision – no matter how amazing that vision is! You need to take action to make it happen:

> *"The vision must be followed by the venture.*
> *It is not enough to stare up the steps -*
> *we must step up the stairs."*
> *(Vance Havner)*

Ask yourself: What little steps do I need to take to achieve my vision? What are the five most important things I need to do *today* to get to my dreams? We can refer to these little steps as our *goals*. It is by achieving our goals that we are able to realise our dream.

This is the part where so many people sabotage themselves. They *do* believe in themselves. They *do* have a fabulous dream... But they don't **DO** anything about it.

Let me give you a personal example...

For years, I had had a desire to go sailing. But that's all it was – a dream. I didn't actually **do** anything about going sailing. I just **wished** I could. Then one day, someone showed me their

sailing holiday photos and, as I walked away from them, I said to myself, "I SO want to do that!" The next morning I woke up with the thought "If I want to have sailing as part of my future, **I** need to **make** it happen."

So I took the first step towards that dream – I started doing research into what sailing courses were available. The next step was to actually book a course. The third step was to inform people I was taking leave. The fourth step was to arrive for the course... and so on.

I had no idea when I started that I was going to end up sailing on privately owned luxury yachts in the Mediterranean for three years. In fact if you had told me that I would be doing that, I would have just laughed and said "No way!" I just took the next step and ended up realising a dream!

Stop Sabotaging yourself!

Do it! Take the steps, one step at a time.

What is crucial to remember here, is...do not put your life on hold while you are taking the steps and trying to achieve your vision. The steps are part of your life. Live now!

This is **your** choice:

> *"I can choose to be happy now,*
> *or I can try to be happy when...or if..."*
> *(Paulo Coelho)*

3. We don't review our plan regularly

By not reviewing our plan regularly, we are not keeping up to date with the changes happening in our lives as we live our dreams. Remember that life is dynamic, not static.

Know that you cannot commit to something forever, because life is not the same forever. You cannot keep attending gym on a Tuesday at 5pm for the rest of your life. Belonging to the moms and tots group is not so cool when your kid is 16!

Your visions will change – and that's fine. Be creative and flexible. Allow for change.

You cannot live the life of your dreams if you are rigid and stuck in an old dream.

When I followed my sailing dream, I had intended to do it for only six months. But when fabulous opportunities presented themselves, I adjusted my plan. I ended up sailing for three years and had some amazing experiences.

After three years, however, I was ready for a new dream - working on luxury yachts was not something I wanted to do forever! Now I am striving towards my goal of becoming an international speaker.

Let me share with you the case of a man I know who is stuck in an old dream…

When he was working as an articled clerk in an accounting firm he was given a beautiful leather briefcase. At the time, he put it away telling himself that he would use it when he passed his Board exam. Well, he failed his board exam and so did not allow himself his reward. He never rewrote the exam and, over twenty years later, he still has not used his briefcase. Everyone else thinks he is a successful businessman - after all he has been financial director of an international company – but he himself believes he is a failure. He still dreams about writing the board exam and using his briefcase. But this is an old dream. He has proved he does not need that qualification, and he has too many new responsibilities (like having a beautiful family) to start studying again, but still it holds him back. Being stuck in his old dream prevents him from moving forward freely toward new dreams and greater success.

Don't sabotage yourself – go with the flow…

> *"The greatest mistake in life is confusing*
> *your dreams with reality.*
> *The greatest tragedy in life is surrendering*
> *your dreams to reality."*
> *(Source unknown)*

A Sabotage-Stopping Summary:

Believe in yourself.

Have a healthy self-esteem. The most important judgement we will ever have to pass in life is the judgement we make on ourselves. Whether you achieve your goals or not depends on your beliefs.

Henry Ford said:

"Whether you think you can or whether you think you can't – you are right."

To achieve your dreams… believe you can!

Make a plan for your own, unique dreams.

Have dreams that are entirely yours based on your *own* values and your *own* purpose. Create your *own* vision - not the vision imposed on you by society, but a vision that is uniquely yours.
Have you taken the time to even think about what you *really* want? If you want to achieve your dreams, you *must* know what they are. You must know what your vision is – for yourself and for your life – and then put that into action by taking the little steps that will get you there.

Review your plan regularly.

Keep up to date with the changes that are happening in your life, as you live your dream. Life is dynamic, not static. Realise that you cannot commit to something forever – life is not the same forever. Your visions will change - and that's absolutely fine. There are no rules. Be creative and flexible. Keep changing what you do as required. Have balance!

Then you can enjoy every minute of the life of your dreams!

In conclusion:
Living the life of your dreams does take time and effort, and many people feel that they don't have the time to do what's necessary. If this *is* what you are telling yourself, the *real* message you're sending out is, "I am not worth spending time on. I am not important enough. Other people, things, or organisations are more important than me."

That message is coming through loud and clear and you believe it!

STOP!
Now is the time for YOU and YOUR dreams.

> *"I am the master of my fate:*
> *I am the captain of my soul."*

(William Ernest Henley, from the poem 'Invictus')

ANSWERING THE CALL

EDDIE BOTES

Eddie Botes is a sought after International speaker, trainer, facilitator and change artist. For almost a decade and a half, Eddie has been inspiring and challenging audiences to think differently in a world that is changing faster than we can imagine.

He has spoken and trained in eight countries with audiences as diverse as corporate executives in multi-national organisations to traditional leaders from some of the most remote locations on the planet.

He is the founder of LeaderShift, an organisation dedicated to developing greatness in leaders and helping organisations manage talent effectively by offering state of the art profiling and assessment tools designed for job match, succession planning, coaching and development.

Eddie is passionate about the pursuit of learning and the gaining of new knowledge. He is a student of the great thinkers and is particularly interested in the changing nature of work and how it will impact on individuals and organisations going into the future.

Tel: (031) 762 3008
Cell: 073 202 7816
eddie@eddiebotes.com
www.eddiebotes.com

ANSWERING THE CALL

Peter Drucker, one of the greatest modern business thinkers made the following statement in an article written nearly ten years ago. "In a few hundred years, when the history of our time will be written from a long-term perspective, it is likely that the most important event historians will see is not technology, not the Internet, not e-commerce. It is an unprecedented change in the human condition. For the first time – literally – substantial and rapidly growing numbers of people have choices. For the first time, they will have to manage themselves. And society is totally unprepared for it."

In the not too distant past, the choices of human beings were vory limited with respect to their choice of career. It was very difficult, if not impossible for individuals to rise above their social standing or class. Jobs and skills were passed down from one generation to the next. Even as recent as the middle of the last century, it was common practice for fathers to insist that their sons follow in their footsteps by becoming bankers or lawyers or doctors.

One of my favourite movies is the 1989 classic "Dead Poets Society". The movie is set in 1959 at an exclusive boys' prep school called Welton Academy in Vermont. It tells the story of a group of boys who are inspired by their new English teacher (Robin Williams) to find their identity and discover and express their unique passion and talent in a world that values conformity and authority. One of the central stories is that of Neil Perry played by Robert Sean Leonard, a gifted and diligent student who discovers his passion for acting and his futile attempts to be accepted and validated by his father who has planned and envisioned every detail of his son's future as a doctor.

When we consider the historical context of the movie set against the backdrop of the Industrial age, it is easy to see how the thinking of the time permeated throughout organisations and institutions of learning. Henry Ford was reputed to have made the following statement a number of decades earlier, "All I want are arms and legs, don't give me whole people". The message in essence was "Don't think, don't be innovative, just do what I am telling you to do". Those in positions of power were paid to think and were perceived as those with the brains. People were taught what to think and not how to think. We created a system where many individuals accepted the political and social premises of their society without ever questioning. The main assets and drivers of economic prosperity in the industrial age were tangibles like machines, brick and mortar - things. Wealth creation was clustered around the physical infrastructure of ports, canals and the railways. People were certainly necessary for the success of an organisation, but could be replaced easily.

All that was wanted were arms and legs. We had no need for hearts, minds and souls. People were just another resource that, like money and machines, needed to be controlled. Organisations had a distinct advantage based on their geographical location, or the products and services that they offered. It was not uncommon for individuals to dedicate their entire lives to serving a single organisation.

We are living in a very different world now. The knowledge worker age has brought with it an unprecedented freedom and capacity for individuals to choose and design their own future. Although the phrase "knowledge worker" was first coined by Peter Drucker in 1959 and the concept spoken about in many publications since, it is generally acknowledged or accepted that 1989 was the real advent of the information age. Modern organisations are becoming more reliant on the ideas, information and intelligence of its people. The market value of modern organisations is often 20, 30, 40 times the value of its fixed assets, the "things" that were the main economic drivers in times past. Although worth less now, Google's value in November of 2007 was over $220 billion, considerably more than its fixed assets. Organisations are nothing more than a collection of key people whose hearts, minds and souls are critically important in our ability to compete in a global market place. Research is showing that the modern worker is looking for more meaning and a greater sense of purpose in the work that they do. They want to feel that they are contributing to something greater than themselves. Loyalty is not something that we can expect from the modern knowledge worker.

Individuals now are changing careers on average at least four times during their lifetime, not jobs, but careers. The work that we do will increasingly not need us to go to a physical location called an office. Mobile offices in the form of a laptop and phone or handheld computer are common practice. It is not unusual for members of a team to work together on a project without ever seeing each other.

What are the implications of all of this for the modern organisation and the individuals that they consist of? Despite the fact that we live in a knowledge worker economy, most businesses still operate from an industrial age mentality with regards how they see and treat people. The vast majority of individuals feel that they are in jobs that do not require or sometimes even allow them to use their knowledge, skills and expertise. They feel micromanaged and feel that their work is largely without meaning. They feel that they have so much more to offer and their bosses are oblivious of their unique talents and gifts.

My father recently retired after dedicating the last forty two years of his life to serving one of South Africa's top four banks. He is a young 63 years old and there had been talk of retirement from the bank's side for a number of years. White males in their fifties are a dying breed in large South African organisations. The dilemma they had was that he was very good at what he does. As a result, he has been preparing for life after the bank by setting up a golf touring business. This required many nights over months to become accredited as a tour operator. There are two reasons that I am sharing this story with you. One would expect that the kind of loyalty and dedication displayed by my father over the last forty two years would in some way be reciprocated. I think a fair retirement package would have been a minimal expectation. In this particular case he was given six months' salary as a retrenchment package and his pension which is now worth 25% less than it was just over a year ago because of the recent collapse of global markets. "Have a nice life, thank you for your contribution". Having said this though, I have seldom seen my father so passionate and filled with creative energy. I could sense his restlessness and frustration over the last number of years at having to grind out a living in an organisation where the bureaucracy and red tape stifled innovation and creativity.

Greed and the pursuit of numbers take precedence over the lives of human beings. Large corporations seem to have lost their way. We can understand the frustration of individuals working in this kind of culture. When the core purpose is to chase numbers you will always have a battle for the hearts, minds and souls of people. The generation entering business now will not stay long in organisations like this. In his 1997 book "The hungry spirit", Charles Handy quotes from a poem by David Whyte: "Always this energy smoulders inside; when it remains unlit the body fills itself with smoke." Handy then gives the following commentary, "An organisation that leaves the individual souls imprisoned and unlit fills itself with smoke. It is not only inefficient, it is indecent. We need the chance in our work, not just in our leisure, to discover the truth about ourselves".

The second point that I wanted to make with regards the story of my father is that he still has many productive years left where he can make a contribution. We are generally healthier than previous generations and are therefore living longer. More and more individuals will be starting their own organisations. I don't know what the South African statistics are but according to recent statistics in the UK, more than 60% of British businesses have only one employee, being the owner, and another 20% have less than five employees. This is going to be a trend as large organisations continue to outsource or subcontract some of their non core functions. The effects of the global economic crisis will contribute to this as organisations have to let go of many individuals. The real social revolution of the last number of decades is that we are moving from a world which is largely organised for us, which admittedly we choose as individuals, to a world in which we are all forced to be in charge of our own destiny.

Peter Druckers' statement applies just as much now as it did ten years ago when he made it. Are we ready as individuals to manage ourselves? Does our educational system prepare us adequately for this kind of world? As all the traditional structures disappear we are going to have to take personal responsibility, and we have to decide upfront what we are all about. This applies just as much to organisations, who are going to have to ask similar questions if they are going to attract and keep the young talented people that are entering business in the 21st century. The increased image of work as a 'rat race' in modern times has led many to question their own attitudes to work and to seek a better alternative; a more harmonious work-life balance. Many believe that long work hours, unpaid overtime, stressful jobs and time spent commuting, less time for family life and/or friends, has led to a generally unhappier workforce and general population who are unable to enjoy the benefits of increased economic prosperity and a generally higher standard of living than was enjoyed by previous generations. There is an increased perception that people in the West are increasingly feeling a sense of existential crisis in their working lives. On the one hand, they are expecting more from their work experience, including that it will nurture personal development and self actualisation. On the other hand, they are finding the capitalist, corporate model of work to be devoid of a sense of soul, lacking in any great sense of meaning.

The generation entering business now has a very different concept of work to their parents. Generation Y as they have come to be known have watched as their parents, the baby boomers worked punishing hours to make money. They have seen how their parents reaped the rewards that came along with that, the cars, the houses and the material wealth. They have benefited from this increased material wealth, being the most materially invested and entertained generation yet. They have also however, been witness to the great cost that their parents have had to pay for their 'success' in terms of broken marriages, absentee parenting and stress related illnesses. For the most part they are disillusioned with the material wealth that they have been part of. This generation don't live to work, they work to live. They have graduated from higher education establishments with the idea that they will not suffer the same fate as the generation before. They are therefore more demanding in terms of how much they ask to be paid, more demanding in the way they want to work, how flexible their hours are and so forth. They seem to understand that a fine balance must be struck between their work and personal life.

The biggest difference for employers is that they are looking for work with much more meaning and significance than before. They are more inclined to want to know what the organisation stands for and what their role in it is and are more likely to look at future progress in an organisation in terms of the contribution that they can make as opposed to the notion of climbing the corporate ladder. As a collective they tend to show a greater sense of social conscience, demonstrated by the growth of service organisations in universities. A generation full of self confidence they want much more than the chance to earn a living, they want attention from their bosses and the chance to offer some benefit to society.

What does this mean for Generation Xers like me, the generation sandwiched between this new wave of bright, young work entrants and the most influential generation in business today, the baby boomers. What does this mean for all of us? How do we cope, compete and thrive in a world that is changing at an ever increasing rate. How do we make sense of this world? Within every one of us there is a need to live a life of significance, to achieve greatness. I think it's fair to say that most of us want to live so that others can live better after we have gone, so that we can achieve some kind of immortality through others. Not many individuals can get really excited about "increasing shareholder value". We feel a sense that there must be more to live for.

Despite all of this longing for a greater sense of meaning, 67% of the working population are in jobs they don't want to be in. They feel stuck, empty, frustrated and feel that their lives are devoid of a sense of purpose. Work seems all about the pursuit of numbers and many are feeling the pressure. Looking to generation Y most are more likely to choose a vocation as opposed to a career. Sam Keen, the noted American author, professor and philosopher once said "A society in which vocation and job are separated for most people gradually creates an economy that is often devoid of spirit, one that frequently fills our pocketbooks at the cost of emptying our souls."

The etymology of the word vocation as opposed to the word career is very interesting. The word vocation comes from the Latin word 'vocare' or 'to call'. It denotes a voice summoning us to a unique purpose. The word career comes from the Latin word 'carrera', which means 'race', and the middle French word for race track. It denotes quickly moving in a circle never going anywhere, the traditional concept of progressing up an ordered hierarchy within an organisation or profession. The increased image of work as a 'rat race' in modern times has led many to question their own attitudes to work and search for a better alternative.

I would like now to take a look at how we can begin to put the wheels in motion and discover a better alternative. I invite you to take a deep, introspective look at your own life and the work that you do and then consider the words of Honore de Balzac, the great French novelist and playwright, "Vocations which we wanted to pursue, but didn't, bleed, like colours, on the whole of our existence."

In his 2001 book "Good to Great", Jim Collins introduced his Hedgehog concept with its three circles.

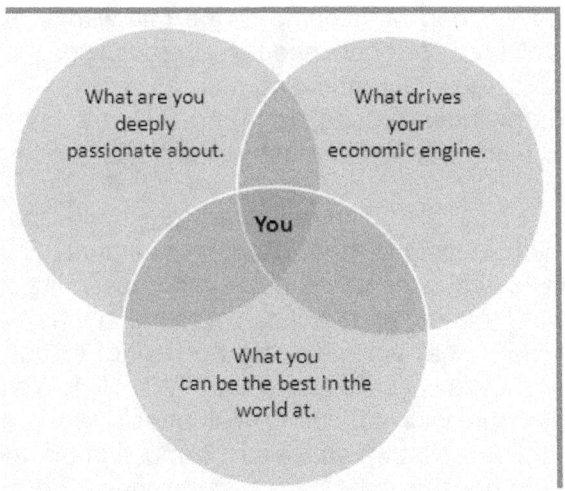

It is at the intersection of the three circles that we can discover our vocation. He suggests that if we can construct a work / life concept that meets the following three tests, then we would have identified our hedgehog concept. Stephen Covey, in his 2004 book "The 8th Habit" expands on this concept which he identifies as 'voice' – our unique personal significance. Covey adds a fourth dimension, conscience. In his words, "When you engage in a work that taps your talent and fuels your passion -

that rises out of a great need in the world that you feel drawn by conscience to meet – therein lies your voice, your calling, your soul's code".

Passion

First, are you doing work that you absolutely love to do? Is this what you are truly passionate about, that which speaks to your most authentic self. We almost get lost in the moment. When we are doing what we love, an hour seems like five minutes, conversely when we are doing things we don't like to do, five minutes can seem like an hour. As we grow up, this true self gets buried by the influence and expectations of family, friends, teachers, and the media. We get sorted and labelled and placed into boxes. Instead of listening to the call within us, we make decisions based on our need for recognition, acceptance, prestige and security. Embracing this call requires us to shut off the voices of those around us telling us what we ought to be doing and being true to our most authentic selves.

We very often are dismissive of our own thoughts and philosophies as insignificant in favour of authority figures whose philosophies we accept without ever questioning. The most difficult part for many of us will be overcoming the obstacles and rationalisations that we make for not following our vocations. Abraham Maslow believed that "We fear our highest possibilities (as well as our lowest ones). We are generally afraid to become that which we can glimpse in our most perfect moments, under the most perfect conditions, under conditions of great courage. We enjoy and even thrill to the godlike possibilities we see in ourselves in such peak moments. And yet we simultaneously shiver with weakness, awe, and fear before these very same possibilities." For those individuals, where passion intersects with their job, there will be no need for supervision. Their motivation, or motive for action is internally derived. It keeps them pressing forward when everything else around them is shouting for them to quit.

Talent

Are you doing work for which you have a genetic or God-given talent for, and is this something that you could potentially become the best in the world at? Our skills are not necessarily our talents. Our talents do however require skills. Talent is an innate ability that is improved with discipline and passion. We may have skills and knowledge in areas that are outside of our talents, but in order to truly harness the power of a true vocation, it requires that we choose something that requires the use of our talents. My oldest son Paul, who is currently twelve years old, has a natural aptitude for music (amongst others). He has the ability to listen to a piece of music and then play it on the piano or guitar. His musical ability on the piano and guitar is largely self taught. Because he loves these instruments, he will sit for hours downloading the chords from the internet and will then work out pieces of music. He is internally motivated to become better and better. He does not need anybody to tell him to practise. His talent and passion have fueled his creativity and driven him to want to start a band with some friends and create something collectively that they could not do individually.

What drives your economic engine?

Need. Is the market place willing to pay you and pay you well for what you do. Is there a need in the world that you can provide a solution for?

Conscience

Vincent van Gogh once said that our conscience is our compass. Human beings generally share an innate moral sense that is a guide for the decisions we make. When we feel drawn by conscience to a certain work the results can be astounding. While on a business trip to Zambia a number of years ago, I met a number of university students who had come to Zambia at their own cost to spend a few weeks to volunteer at an orphanage that had been founded to care for children who had lost parents to AIDS. I enquired as to how they had come to hear of this organisation. I was told that it was started by an

American woman who after visiting Zambia some years ago and seeing the devastating effect that the disease was having on the country, was moved to start a charity. From very humble beginnings they recently purchased a 50 hectare piece of land on the outskirts of the city where they are building a comfortable facility for these children.

They employ a full time staff compliment and have a steady flow of volunteer college students who arrive every few weeks to replace those that leave. The founder spends a number of months there each year and has a vision to eventually relocate to Zambia and be permanently involved. She started this organisation after seeing a great need in the local community and after being drawn by conscience to act upon that need. Hundreds of children now benefit from this act and over the years scores of college students, some who had never been outside of sub-urban America have had their world view expanded and been prompted to continue in looking outside of thomselves to make a greater difference in the world.

In this, the 21st century, where we have choices like never before in the history of the world, there is absolutely no reason why we should not be doing work that is meaningful and fulfilling to us. We can live the lives that we spend a lot of time dreaming about. Henry David Thoreau once said "Most men lead lives of quiet desperation and go to the grave with the song still in them". Let us not resign ourselves to this type of oxistence, let us break out and dare to find new ground. I wish you luck on your journey.

GROW YOUR BUSINESS

IAN RHEEDER

From humble beginnings, Ian has clawed himself to the top of his industry. In 2003 he qualified as a Chartered Marketer (CM), the highest professional marketing qualification recognised both in South Africa and Europe. Ian is also a registered training Assessor with Services SETA South Africa, who is registered to facilitate almost all their marketing and sales programmes. He has facilitated marketing and sales management at the Gordon Institute of Business Science (GIBS) since 2007, and is currently part of the GIBS adjunct faculty.

Besides working with top brands, Ian facilitates over 30 self-authored programmes at leading business schools. He describes himself as a 'markoholic' and one of SA's most passionate marketing speakers. (Ian has hundreds of brilliant references to back this up.) In October 2009 he was voted the best speaker at an international marketing conference and in 2010 was nominated the Johannesburg Chapter President of the Professional Speakers Association (PSASA).

Tel: (011) 447 0271
Cell: 083 300 8080
ian@markitects.co.za
www.makitects.co.za

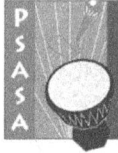

GROW YOUR BUSINESS

Without clear goals, a strategy is just a wish, which is why a strategic sales plan has deadlines with specific tasks for specific people.

However, putting a strategic sales plan together is no easy task, particularly if there are tight deadlines involved and the CEO (rightly) insists that you don't achieve your sales growth via the simple strategy of slashing prices!

A tried-and-tested approach – of great value when you feel under pressure and likely to miss some vital step in the process – is to fall back on the Ansoff Growth Matrix. Although in existence since the 1950s, it remains a good framework for ensuring that you methodically cover all your bases as you decide the direction your sales team should take.

The four options (see picture on next page) should always form the heart of the detailed tactical sales plan. But a word of warning before you proceed: while the matrix is a framework, it's not a panacea for all the ills of the sales department, or indeed the business. Instead, sales managers must continuously research, innovate and implement this four-pronged growth strategy according to their own needs and changing market conditions.

Source: Based on Professor Ansoff's Harvard Business Review article (Sep/Oct, 1957, pp.113-124)

Growth Strategies

	Present Products	New Products (NPD)
Present or Existing Markets	**Market Penetration.** Growth in <u>existing</u> product Markets. 1. Increase market **Share (cross-sell and/or up-sell)** 2. Increase product **Usage** ➤ Increased **Frequency** used ➤ Increased **Quantity** used ➤ Find **New Application** for current users	New **Product Development (NPD)** Develop **New products** for the **Same** market 1. Add product **Features** 2. Develop a **New-generation** product (iPod, L.E.D. TV)
New Markets	New **Market Development** 1. Expand geographically 2. Target new segments	**Diversification** Involving <u>new</u> products and <u>new</u> markets 1. Related (Coffee to hot chocolate) 2. Unrelated (Cars to motorbikes)

Vertical Integration, Mergers, Acquisitions, Strategic Alliances
Forward, Backward and/or Horizontal Integration - (non-organic growth)

Major growth decisions using the Matrix

The above model is designed to grow a business into existing and new segments, with existing and new products or services. For example, targeting new markets with present services is market development, while targeting new markets with new services is diversification.

Where both the product and market is understood, market penetration is the least risky. But where the product and market is not yet tested, diversification is the most risky.

Tactical sales plan using the matrix

A tactical sales plan is part of the broader sales strategy, but identifies the people responsible for achieving the budgeted sales units, turnover, profit and activities. As part of this process, it's crucial that daily, weekly, monthly and quarterly goals are agreed upon.

This plan has two key elements:

a). Existing market growth strategies and tactics (Market Penetration & New Product Development in the Ansoff Matrix).

Tactical detail here will include answers to the following questions: 'who'; 'what'; 'where'; 'when'; 'why', and 'what happens thereafter'. For example, you may decide that you will exceed quota with existing customers by doing the following:

* Increasing share of key customers by launching x-number of new products/services per annum for existing and possible cross-border markets.

* Sending out y-number of white papers to your customer base on topics which interest them.

* Once a new customer is satisfied with their first delivery, you will ask for the names of x-number of associates who may be interested in your product/service.

b). New business acquisition strategies & tactics (New Market Development & Diversification in the Ansoff Matrix).

You may decide you will meet or exceed quotas by implementing the following tactics (for example):

* Research x-number of new prospects in a specific region before launching your new products/services.

* Join y-number of associations which are used and respected by your prospects.

* Visit a specified number of trade shows frequented by key decision makers.

* Do x-number of public talks on a topical and well-researched subject.

Downturn sales management

Remember, the ideal sales strategy blends both strategic and tactical elements, and also takes cognisance of the other strategies of the business, including marketing. Slavishly following the Ansoff Matrix will not provide a sales manager with a ready-made set of strategic answers – but it will provide a hefty nudge in the right directions.

Integration as a strategy

Based on my own experience, I have added a fifth growth strategy – integration – to the four used by the late, great Professor Ansoff in his Matrix.

Integration enables non-organic growth via new business acquisitions and/or partnerships, and a crucial benefit is that it allows a business to take control of the value chain and improve innovation, quality and availability. Four integration options exist:

Backward integration is taking over command of your upstream supply-chain. This is done by buying out your supplier or becoming a producer of your product or service.

Forward integration (also known as dis-intermediation) is taking control of your downstream channel-to-market. Cutting out the middleman can increase profit margins, and if done well, also improves service through superior account coordination and strategic partnering.

Vertical integration is implementing both backward and forward integration. An excellent example of this is the global zipper giant, YKK. It sources its own raw materials, produce the machines that manufacture the zippers and, finally, sells the products using its own sales force. While the benefit is a high performance value chain, the downside of vertical integration is that it is capital intensive, almost always requiring taking a step backwards before advancing forwards.

Horizontal integration is the merger with a company similar to yours, offering economies-of-scale and cherry-picked resources.

Although not a sales strategy in the true sense, successful integration can bring about many benefits for the sales team – including more selling opportunities and greater control over product quality and delivery schedules.

Remember that the sales force is the sharp tip of the pencil; mess with them in a recessionary climate and you mess up the entire business writing instrument. A sales manager's most important job is to improve her team's morale, not achieve sales targets. Achieving objectives is just a by-product of energised and focused salespeople.

Thus a sales manager's responsibility should be to focus on two main areas, motivating and developing their sales team In a downturn, sales managers need to become even stronger leaders, yet the main reason for a salesperson's resignation is still "my boss".

In a recent Harvard Business Review article the following factors, in order of importance, were responsible for employee satisfaction: the job itself, training, pay, advancement fairness, treatment with respect and dignity, teamwork and the company's interest in employee well-being. Notice that training was cited second.

1. Motivating Salespeople through Development

Behaviour is not random, it's caused; and at different career stages a salesperson has different needs. A top salesperson knows her worth and doesn't want to be held back from further development. Sales people will also compare their treatment to that of 'equitable others' (Adams' Equity Theory). If treatment is perceived to be inequitable, they will become de-motivated. Performers have an intense drive to win and thrive on the possibility of impacting on the performance of their organisation. However in a slump, their earning potential may have declined; so by increasing their territory and field of responsibility, their morale and self-esteem is reignited. Customers sense this motivation, and it has a deep influence on their purchasing decisions. Here are a few more ideas to develop your team:

A top sales manager should spend about 30% of their day selling with their team and doing on-the-job coaching. This engagement leads to less staff turnover and increased customer satisfaction. Engagement not only allows you to keep a finger on the market's pulse and crack more deals, but also allows you to lead by example. Imagine how well you could chair your sales meetings if you did this? This hands-on approach motivates salespeople by giving them regular feedback and directs effort by highlighting which products should receive the most attention. It provides standards for performance evaluation and allows the manager to focus on staff that are under performing on the three different types of sales quotas/sales volume, profit/GP% and/or activities. Managers can then go on calls with these top or under-performers to observe their techniques.

Your job and career may depend on understanding the psychology of your salespeople – what drives them at different career stages? Always be alert for top performers who have a desire to move to the next level, and realistically design a career path for them. Top salespeople love a challenge and the opportunity to perform.

To improve their ability, always determine everyone's specific formal training needs. Empower the experienced member, and get them to use their superior skills to develop the rest of the team. Recognise top performers by awarding them with prizes or gifts at your official recognition awards evening. Well executed, sales managers should also be rewarded for developing their team.

2. Motivation through Leadership

A feeble knee-jerk reaction to a downswing is to drive your staff harder. Whatever you do, getting people motivated to implement your new exciting vision requires strong leadership. Don't forget that the formula for performance = opportunity x ability x motivation. But in reality too many sales managers are consumed by administration; in a recession they need to integrate themselves back into the sales force to influence and inspire their actions – through personal demonstration, this will reignite a winning atmosphere to tackle change in a challenging economic climate. Leading by example also gives the sales manager legitimate, expertise and relating/friendship power.

Spend time strategising and planning with your team. Tap into your salespeople and customers' minds to find the best opportunities. This research will equate to the right downturn product range and thus improve your competitive advantage.

By group consensus, get your entire team to buy-in to a new compelling vision for the sales department. Once all have endorsed the new way forward, write up your detailed mission of how to achieve it. To mobilise the entire team, objectives must be strategically meaningful - this value congruence of everyone striving for the same core purpose and objectives, is motivational and empowering to the team.

Be careful of too much internal competition vs. cooperation amongst sales folk. In her book Hot Spots, "Why some companies buzz with energy and innovation – and others don't" (2007), Lynda Gratton easily convinces us that a too highly individually incentivised employee will be tempted to knowledge hoard and not co-operate with the team. It's therefore apparent after reading her book that sales managers need to cleverly incentivise the team too. It's not all about great individuals, but great relationships between great people.

3. Change Management is Crucial in a Downturn

"The pessimist complains about the wind; the optimist expects it to change; the realist adjusts the sails." (William Ward).

One study estimated that less than 10% of strategies are effectively implemented. Another study revealed that CEOs mistakenly believed that their failure was due to bad strategy, but in reality 70% of the CEO's just did not implement the strategy. Not surprisingly, it's estimated that only 20% of employees are change-friendly, 50% are 'fence sitters' and 30% resist change and will even attempt to make the sales manager's initiative fail. A recent global study of 3623 managers indicates that 40% of executives are resistant to change during a stressful recession - this is probably because about 30% of executives are not equipped to execute change, mainly due to their reluctance to attend training. So then how will you get your staff to buy-in, let alone implement the solution? The sales manager must be trusted - but trust, like respect, is earned. Top sales managers know the ropes and can show the others the swinging maneuvers - they've been there and can now confidently show the way.

So here's the plan. Firstly, the new environment must be assessed, and the strategy redesigned. The team should be skilled up, and the sales process redesigned inline with redefined customer segments. The next step is to find measurement metrics (sales volume, profit targets and activities) against which to evaluate the change-programmes' success. The sales manager should then develop new sales support initiatives to support the change. Examples include: strategic sessions, training (i.e. key account management and negotiation skills), coaching, meaningful incentives, and team selling tactics. Finally implementation should start with a pilot test programme. Once there is buy-in to the change programme, the successful pilot programme can be rolled out nationally. But remember that a leader keeps their followers' 'chins-up' – excited about the vision; and a manager keeps their 'chins-down' – energised to implement the mission. Thus you need to know when to lead and when to manage.

NOT THE SHORTCUT TO SALES SUCCESS

Why 'The Secret' to sales success is so misleading. Books like The Secret* argue that positive thoughts are enough to achieve success. I believe successful salesmanship requires more. Whether leading a sales team or a country – everything counts. To isolate just one big concept and call it 'the secret' is not just dangerous, it's an omission. It is this omission which makes me want to share what successful managers do to ensure their success and that of their sales teams. Visualisation, or focus, is just part of 'the secret' to success. What many books on the topic do not emphasise is just how much energy, hard work, determination, self-discipline, persistence, and courage are required to achieve your organisation's sales goals. Thomas Edison, who often worked 40 hours without sleep, was no fool when he said "Genius is 1% inspiration and 99% perspiration".

In the chapter How to Use The Secret, The Secret recommends the following: "The Creative Process helps you create what you want in three simple steps: ask, believe and receive." (p.68). This is partly correct, what it's missed out is the all important, detailed strategic plan of action, before you "receive". Secondly, the same chapter also stipulates "You do not have to ask over and over again. Just ask once. It is exactly like placing an order from a catalogue." (p.48). But in reality, success requires persistent daily attention (asking) and action.

By playing on people's greed, insecurity and lack of responsibility, it's easy to get a populace believing in 'quick fixes' to achieve their goals. By avoiding reasonable logic and only choosing to focus on the one-in-a-million random statistic, these folk can convince themselves that shortcuts do exist. This new-age 'get-success-quick' mindset clearly played a role in the current global credit crisis, with its unprecedented acts of corruption and desire to make money without labour. "The Secret", or believing is just the first project. In the real world the next project is a "Plan of Action", followed by actually acting out the plan.

Don't be erroneously led into believing there's a shortcut to a sales team's success either. Thoughts are not a plan; a plan is not action.

Energy or Focus: **Which is best?**
Hypothetically, choose only one for the rest of your life?

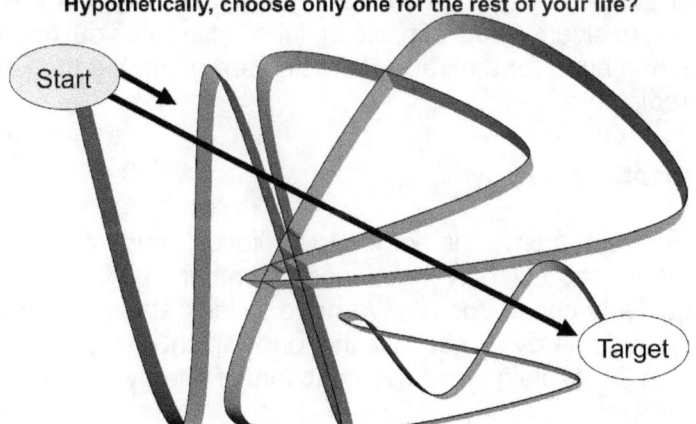

The short arrow is just "focus"; you'll just stare at the target. The squiggly line is just energy; a lot of wasted energy, but better than just "focus". The long arrow is a great combination of both "energy" and "focus".

Defining Success

Defining 'success' is a personal thing. During my sales training programmes I've asked hundreds of audiences this question: If they were forced to choose only one of the following two characteristics to achieve success – **energy** or **focus** – which would they choose? The majority always chose **focus.**

The reason for choosing 'focus' is twofold – it's what society and books like The Secret* have taught us, and it's easier to not act. Remember, the audiences were forced to choose either 'energy' or 'focus'. The 'focus' majority were then left seated to do exactly this, whilst the 'energy' minority were allowed to get up and do **anything**. It then swiftly dawned upon the seated majority that they are just leaving indentations on their seats, whilst the minority – even though blindfolded – were clearly discovering new avenues through their actions.

It is through this exploration of 'energised action' that sales managers will naturally select what works and what doesn't. Peter Drucker, author of 39 management books, puts it across so persuasively: "You can either take action or you can hang back and hope for a miracle. Miracles are great, but they are so unpredictable."

Concepts of Energy

The correct answer is, of course, 'focus' **and** 'energy'; but forced to choose only one, most members of the audience misguidedly chose 'focus'. We need to look at five concepts of using our energy – not just the one which involves focused thinking. To explain these five concepts of energy, imagine a hot air balloon:

Self-Worth Energy

To elevate yourself to the altitude you desire, the hot air balloon must be **large enough**. This is your genuine inner self-esteem, filled with positive and unruffled feelings. Please note that a dysfunctional, narcissistic, overestimation of oneself is not a healthy self-esteem. Self-worth must be grounded in real business competence and sales skills, not just wishful illusory thinking or screaming out "yes, yes, yes" during sales meetings.

Emotional Energy (Subconscious Mind)

We use both the subconscious and conscious mind for making decisions. This 'whole brain' is responsible for everything, from healthy customer relationships to how we act. Feelings – like the deeply rooted 'gut' feel of self-worth, happiness and gratitude – are more important than thoughts. Why? Because healthy feelings are loaded with potent energy.

These feelings, which are observable on a brain scanner, can literally override reason. Like a light switch they'll turn you on or off, or comfort you whilst delivering a sales presentation. The exciting thing is, with every new brain scan study, it's becoming clear how our subconscious guides our intuition and actions. Of course, when you are aware of how your brain system works, miracle moments jump out at you all the time. It's miraculous to be alive when you start witnessing your new consciousness unfold.

Mental Energy (Conscious Mind)

Using our conscious 'front-burner', we may rationally decide to steer hot energised air into our subconscious balloon. We need to responsibly and consciously generate positive thoughts, as negative thoughts are cold air – causing the balloon to barely fill and never take off.

Physical Energy

Neuroscientist, Brian Knutson, has proven that action is its own reward. Action, the part of success that The Secret book almost totally ignores, really is the best way of emotionally re-programming, learning new feelings, or un-learning deeply-seated feelings of inadequacy in the sales arena. It's so healing that happiness can be described simply as **goal directed engagement**. Put another way: the thrill of the hunt is more enjoyable than the pleasure of the feast. It's a fact - as human beings, we're just hardwired in this manner.

If you consciously slow your breathing, it immediately makes you feel less anxious – hence, action changes our mood and thought. We also feel better after a gym workout. Writing out a gratitude list is more rewarding and mood-lifting than just thinking about a list. Therefore, 'action' is not just an act but a spiritual awakening – it is emotional therapy refuelling us so that we can act again. In sales terms: instead of thinking about it, we need to learn to just pick up the phone, make an appointment and present our offer.

Success Energy

The 'pleasure of the feast' is landing your craft at the destination of choice, creating a pleasurable mood that refuels and reignites the success-loop. For example, the best time to close another sales deal is right after closing the previous one.

Sloth, not lack of vision, is one of the seven deadly sins. Thus, after all is said and done, action would have counted the most.

* Published in 2006 as both a book and DVD, The Secret is based on the Law of Attraction. In essence, it proposes that anything which happens to you, or comes to you, is the result of your thoughts. What you focus on will come about as you train your thoughts on its attraction. Written by Australian Rhonda

Byrne, it sold millions of copies worldwide and attained cult status. The Secret also spawned other inspirational books like Shortcut to Miracle, How to Change Your Consciousness and Transform Your Life. Written by Michael C. Rann and Elizabeth Rann Arrott, both of whom have extensive backgrounds as sales and advertising executives, the book attempts to not only describe how the Law of Attraction works, but to show how to apply it to the challenges of daily life.

Setting Sales Quotas

Do you know what the three main sales performance areas are to track?

Of all the promotional tools, face-to-face selling is the most costly to reach your target audience, but done well, it's also the most cost effective vehicle. But, the sales function has changed so dramatically over the last couple of decades that a sales manager trained in the 1990s needs to forget some old tricks and learn a few new ones. Apart from the style of selling having changed from high-pressure tactics to a more high-trust style, technology needs to be embraced to compete with more techno-savvy global competitors. To improve the sales process, technology applications include the intelligent use of CRM, account planning, quota allocation, forecasting and pipeline management. Interestingly though, adopting this new technology is why it takes a new sales consultant so long to be productive, but once they're trained, they fly. The change has been so radical that Rick Canada at Motorola says "The traditional sales force is a dinosaur – a remnant of past success."

Being accountable for the top-line, the Chief Sales Officer (CSO) must design and redesign the organisation to match the sales and marketing strategy. The CSO needs to have a firm grip on the entire organisation's business plan and understand how each function operates. When you think about it, a hands-on sales manager is also the most likely person to feed the executive team with the most valuable customer insights. Selling is therefore no longer a single function mindset, but the department needs to work extremely closely with everyone in the customer-facing team. In a customer-centric organisation a sales manager should be skilled enough to collaborate with all departments. Today's successful sales managers and sales people should really be marketers that have as much information to assist them to offer a complete solution. Recent surveys recommend that a business-to-business sales person should really see themselves as management consultants who sell a complete solution that is much wider than their product range. For example, landing a new key account is usually the easy 'selling' part; it's the marriage after the honeymoon period that is much more challenging which needs to be monitored. A key account manager should for example have service level targets and be alert to cross-selling and up-selling to loyal customers.

In their featured article, "The Ultimately Accountable Job" Jerome Colletti and Mary Fiss recommends: "At least 15% of a Chief Sales Officer's time should be spent establishing and communicating a clear course for accomplishing the current year's business plan. Sales will always be the ultimately accountable job. No other function bears such exposed responsibility for delivering on the numbers." Once you have a motivated team, knowing what targets to aim for will dramatically improve your strategic prowess as a sales manager. Knowing what their quotas are and how to achieve them will also further motivate the sales team. So what are the three main sales performance quotas to track?

1. Sales Volume Quotas

When a sales force does not have control of the profit margins they sell at, a popular target is sales volume. Volumes can be tracked by either total rand value and/or units sold. If your product range is strongly affected by the oil price or the exchange rate, then unit sales are appropriate to track. If the selling price is fixed, then definitely track sales rand value.

2. Profit-based Quotas

When sales people have control over the price they negotiate, and also have a wide range of solutions to sell into a market, the sales manager needs to carefully track and incentivise selling at the highest possible price. Because of profit margins being squeezed during a recession, a combination of both profit and sales volume is popular to track.

3. Activities Quotas

Daily, weekly, monthly and quarterly activities, which produce future results, can be tracked to get the lazy sales person to do what needs to be done. Typical activities for 'hunters' and 'farmers' would be the number of calls, proposals, installations, service calls and demonstrations performed. A word of warning though, these activities may be done in a mere 'tick-the-box' fashion, and thus may not result in sales targets being met, so a triangulation of all three quotas is necessary. Service feedback has also fast become a standard 'quota' to track for a key account manager's performance appraisal. Michael E. Porter, the celebrated strategist and Harvard Business School Professor highlights that 'activities' are the bridges between strategy and implementation.

That is to say, activities are the secret bridges between a plan in your head and desired results. But beware – adults also want to know why they do certain activities. Any activity that is forced upon an employee should easily be linked back to the overarching sales strategy and their personal sales targets; this way a salesperson can manage their targets and be in control of their performance bonus. If there's a direct line of sight between everything they do and their quotas, they tend to do it.

In closing, remember that behaviour is not random; it's caused. Be careful of targets that are too individualistic, but remember to run the sales force as a team. Whatever quota you choose, keep motivating your team by giving them regular feedback; go on sales calls with those who are above quota and share your findings with those who are below quota.

EDGE OF THE RAIN

JACQUES DE VILLIERS

Jacques de Villiers (AKA The Business Generator) is a professional speaker specialising in marketing, Internet marketing, public relations and sales.

He started out on his own in 1998 with a speakers bureau called Motivators International. He sold it in 2007 to run his marketing agency, MindTrust Marketing full time.

He gets asked to present at conferences from time-to-time. The two keynotes that are most popular are:

How to Persuade Anybody to do Almost Anything.
Google and the Art of Dating Angelina Jolie.

When he is not speaking and training, you'll find him generating business for his clients through his marketing and sales processes.

Cell: 082 906 3693
jacques@jacquesdevilliers.com
www.jacquesdevilliers.com

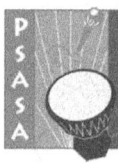

EDGE OF THE RAIN

I spent many a Christmas holiday on my grandfather's farm in Loeriesfontein, 100 kilometres from Calvinia. The farm was typical of most farms in the hot and dusty rain-deprived Karoo. It was unrelenting, unyielding and fit only for sheep, ostriches and the toughest human. Not much grew on it except quinces, the hardiest of weeds and the crustiest of shrubs. When I looked at my grandfather, the craggy lines spidering across his face told the story of hardship and suffering. And, sometimes in an unguarded moment, he'd drop his pose and let me look into his piercing blue eyes and into his soul. Even at a young age I could fathom the undercurrents that ripped through his soul – potential, hopefulness, big dreams, regret, hopes dashed, dreams downscaled and sorrow for potential unfulfilled.

I remember sitting on the veranda with him at the end of a hard day's work (him, not me – I had a relatively carefree time on the farm). We were watching the sun set over the majesty that is the Karoo. He sat with a brandy and coke and a cigarette dangling from his lips and me, sipping home-made ginger beer. This was a time for reflection for him. Sometimes when we sat together, we'd see a wall of rolling dark clouds flooding out sheets of rain, 50 kilometres away as the crow flies. It seemed to fence us in, the lightning strikes keeping us corralled in our little space in the world.

Every so often a couple of errant raindrops carried by a gulf stream wind would splutter onto the veranda. This would give my grandfather cause to look up to the heavens with hope in his heart that the rain would finally bless his farm and his family. Almost every time his hopes were dashed as the rain disappeared like a mirage in a desert. He'd look into his glass, sigh and take another sip of brandy. The drink and smoke at the end of a day's work seemed like his only pleasure in life. That, and playing rummy with me after church on a Sunday.

My grandfather's farm was a typical Karoo farm, on the edge of the rain. His farm had massive potential to grow any number of crops. But the rain fell just out of reach from where he farmed. He knew that if the rain would just fall on his farm, it would be an outstanding success. But, it seemed that he was always destined to be at the edge of the rain, never able to claim the riches and success that were rightfully his.

I'm not saying that there was never any success. There were islands of happiness that popped up in a sea of struggle. Then everyone was excited. Grandmother could buy a new dress from the shop and not have to make her own. I could go to the local shop and buy real sweets. A delightful change from the dried fruit that was my sweet staple! These islands of success and happiness were rare and fleeting. But those rare and fleeting moments were vital to grandfather's survival. They gave him hope and kept him in the game. And because of those moments he never gave up on his family and on his goals, as downscaled as they were. He died at the plough, bent but never broken.

If I sound uncharitable to my grandfather, I'm not. I admired him greatly for his gentleness, dogged determination, sense of duty and wisdom. He may not have been the "classic" success story. But, he left me with a value system that I carry with me today.

Many of my beliefs today are as a result of his guidance and forbearance. Here are some examples that may or may not resonate with you.

Listen to your elders...
　　　　　they might just have something to teach you.

Boy, did I learn this humbling lesson the hard way. My grandfather warned me not to enter the neighbour's farm. The problem was that to get to our farm, I'd have to walk two kilometres. To cut across the neighbour's farm would knock off a good kilometre and a half. It wasn't a problem most days as I was young, fit and bursting with energy. But, on this particular day, I'd spent too much time in the sun and hadn't taken in enough fluids. The sun leached the energy out of me.

I figured I'd cut across the neighbour's farm and buy myself some time so that I could get to a cool drink quicker. I hopped the fence. Halfway across I met an ostrich. A male. As it turns out, he took me for a female ostrich and started strutting his stuff – fluffing feathers and making unearthly noises. He bounded towards me and when he realised I wasn't a willing female, he kicked me so hard that he knocked the wind out of me. I ended up under an excuse for a bush in the harsh sun. He kept a sentinel watch over me and wouldn't allow me to escape. After an hour of this I was getting seriously sunburned and dehydrated.

Luckily for me, a farmer came across me and my predicament. He shooed the ostrich away and took me home. After hydrating me and sorting out my sunburn, I got the hiding of my life. But, it is a lesson I'll never forget.

Every action has a consequence

Everyone on the farm was skilled at using a rifle. As a sapling of a boy, I was only allowed to use a pellet gun and was only allowed to shoot at tins or bottles far out of harm's way. After watching the men hunt Springbok, I was chomping at the bit to prove my "manhood" as well. Of course, I was never going to be allowed to hunt a Springbok for some time to come. I could barely manage the pellet gun, never mind the larger ordinance it took to knock over a buck.

One day, out of sheer frustration and simple bloody-mindedness, I took aim at a bird with the pellet gun. All the tin shooting paid off and I killed it. As luck would have it, my grandfather came past just as I'd done the deed. I had disobeyed him and thought I'd get a serious thrashing. This time he did something different. And, I'm so glad he did because it taught me a valuable lesson that I have carried with me ever since. He said, "Wait here." The waiting was the worst and I imagined every bad thing that could possibly happen to me. He came back about 10 minutes later carrying a ladder. He put the ladder against the tree from which I'd shot the bird. "Climb," he said. With some trepidation, I climbed not knowing what he had in store for me. When I got to the top of the ladder I came upon a nest. In that nest were three chicks with their mouths wide open... waiting for food. Food that would never come because I'd ended the life of their mother.

My grandfather just looked at me with those wise eyes and didn't say anything. He didn't have to. That day I realised that every action has a consequence. There was a kind of a happy ending. I reared the chicks until they took flight. So, at least I managed to salvage some good out of a bad situation that I'd created.

Care for your fellow man

There were times when a worker or a member of his family fell ill. Both my grandfather and grandmother would sit whole evenings helping out until the person was healed. They realised we are all in this game of life together. And, only by helping each other can we help ourselves. Watching the two of them fuss and fret over a little child taught me that every one deserves a bit of gentleness. And, that small acts of kindness could make big difference. As a result my grandfather had fewer problems with his staff than the average farmer in the region – who were a bit more uncharitable when it came to their workers' problems.

Share knowledge

The children on the farm were involved in all aspects of its running. We learned how to cook, how to shear sheep, how to collect water, how to skin an animal, how to preserve fruit and countless other things that were important to the survival of all of us. Knowledge was freely shared so that if one of us faltered, the other could pick up the slack and make sure that things ran smoothly. This ensured that things ran smoothly and that we all survived and thrived.

The best and most pleasant vehicle for our learning was storytelling. After dinner and after the compulsory Bible reading, my grandfather would settle in and tell us stories. He had the ability to weave a lesson into each story so that we could walk away with just a bit more knowledge (and power) than we had before. I learned many lessons from my grandfather and farming in the harshest of terrains. Thinking back on my time on the farm and with my grandfather, I wondered why, like my grandfather, some of us have lives that are harsh and devoid of any real success. It has occurred to me that many of our lives are like that Karoo farm.

We're on the edge of the rain. We can see and taste the rewards that life offers us. We just can't seem to get them, can we? We know that we have all the potential in the world. We know that if we step out of the desert into the rain, we'll get the sustenance we need to succeed. Most of us never get into the rain, do we? It's almost as if we're boxing above our weight class. We go through the motions, slogging and slaving, hoping for that break that will change our lives forever. Our squandered potential fuels our disappointment even further leading us to live lives of quiet desperation.

Have you ever asked yourself why it is that even though you work yourself to the bone and do things right, you still don't get the life you want and deserve? It must have occurred to you that there must be an easier way.

I've posed four questions that I hope will raise an internal debate in you and get you to pay attention. You and I know it is when you don't pay attention to what's happening in your life that you feel serious pain.

You don't know why you're here

To get absolute clarity in your life, you need to know what your purpose is on this earth. You've got to start living on purpose. Too many of us have no idea what we are meant to do with our lives and leave ourselves open to the vagaries of fate. You may be one of those souls that finds it exciting to live in a whimsical fashion, with unpredictability as your partner every day. It's just not a great strategy to help you find direction in your life. Because once you know who you are, what you stand for and what you'll accept and not accept, life becomes a lot simpler. Your purpose can become your North Star, always guiding you in the right direction.

How do I find my purpose, you may ask? That's not an easy one, is it? You've got to spend time with yourself and take a deep, introspective look at who you are and how you want to contribute. Here's the nub of any purpose statement – your purpose is not to be happy. Your purpose is to make a difference in the lives of those around you. Because, it is only when you are making a real difference do you become truly happy.

I cannot stress enough how important it is to discover your purpose first before embarking on any kind of goal-setting exercise. Once you have your purpose all your goals will fall into alignment.

My purpose is: To help people live lives of adventure, destiny and purpose through my God-given talents of thinking, writing and speaking. I fulfill my destiny by inspiring people through my blogs, my writing, my keynote addresses, my seminars and my books. Every goal I set is aimed at achieving my purpose.

When I make a difference in the lives of my family, friends and clients, I'm happy, fulfilled and contented.

Finding your purpose gives you the "why?" One of the biggest motivators in your life is to have a "reason why?" Why am I doing this? Why is this important to my family? Why is this important to my clients? Why is this important to my country? Viktor E. Frankl in his book, Man's Search For Meaning made a strong case for having a "reason why?" Frankl, an Austrian neurologist and psychiatrist was incarcerated in the Nazi concentration camps. He decided to study why some of the inmates seemed to succumb quickly and why others survived in one of the harshest and most inhumane environments ever devised by man. The short answer is that those that survived the Nazi concentration camps had a "reason why?" They had an overriding goal that kept them going. It may have been to see their children again, to stay alive to bring their Nazi jailers to justice or any of a dozen reasons.

You don't know what you want

Once we have a "reason why?"... we need to find ways of achieving it. The reality is that most of us don't really know what we want. We think we do, sort of. It is normally some kind of fuzzy Utopian ideal, isn't it? I want more money. I want to be happy. I want a nice house. I want a beautiful car. I want to live at the coast or in the mountains or maybe Monaco. I want a great relationship with someone who'll love me. I just want to be happy. And so on. It is exactly this kind of fuzzy, non-specific thinking that will get you less than desirable results. Until you get clear on what it is you really want, you'll always be at the edge of the rain. You have to get real and specific about what it is you want. Once you crack that code the rain edges nearer to you.

How do you get clear on what it is you really want? Pick a day and closet yourself away from any interruptions – mobile phone, family, friends and work. Pretend that you have unlimited time and money. What would you do? What would you buy? Who would you meet? What car do you want? Write down a dream list. Don't be judgmental and say, "I couldn't get that". Just write it down.

Once you've got your list, categorise it into short and long-term goals. I want to retire with R5-million cash in the bank is a long-term goal. I want to lose exactly 10 kilograms is a short term goal. Then, set SMART goals to achieve (specific, measurable, achievable, relevant (to your purpose) and time-based).

You don't believe that you deserve success

I believe that the biggest obstacle keeping us at the edge of the rain is that we don't believe that we are worthy of success and happiness. At the heart of this lies our self-image and self-esteem. You've probably heard it more than a dozen times in your life, "Success is an inside job." Well, it's true, isn't it?

I'll put it to you that whatever the circumstances in your life right now, you've created it. In fact, you're exactly where you're supposed to be right now. Your self-esteem and self-image are thermostats that regulate the temperature of your life. When you go above your perceived potential and worth, your thermostat will drop the temperature to what it has been set at. Let's say that 100 degrees is super hot (equate that with wealth, happiness, success, health and the like) and 0 degrees is really cold (equate that with failure and misery). Let's say that you peg yourself at 50 degrees. If you do this you'll always get 50 degrees results. If you go over the 50 degree mark, to let's say, 60 degrees, your thermostat will kick in and drop you back down to 50 degrees... your expectation zone and comfort zone. And when you get back into the zone, you're happy aren't you?

The results aren't exactly what you want, but they're results that fit into your view of the world and the value you place on yourself.

Let me give you an example. Imagine that you earn R5 000 a month. You decide to try your luck at a casino and win R5 000. That's amazing and can really help you. Guess what? Your car breaks down and you have to repair it. Guess how much it costs? That's right... R5 000. Your thermostat kicked in and brought you down to the level of your belief. Until you start getting a serious belief that you are worthy of success, you'll always start getting the same results. I can't say it better than Proverbs 23:7, "As a man thinks in his heart, so is he."

I've always battled at differentiating between self-image and self-esteem until I came across a book by James Arthur Ray called Harmonic Wealth. Ray says that self-image is the way you think about yourself and your world. Self-esteem tells us how we feel about ourselves and our lives.

Other people helped script your self-image. Most of the scripting happened in childhood, didn't it? It has been said that from babyhood to around six years old we're in a brainwave state called Alpha. In this state we absorb information like a sponge.

Who did we hang out with up until six? Our parents.
Whether we like it or not, our parents are largely responsible for the way we turned out, aren't they? Whatever they told you, you absorbed and believed. If you had empowering parents who were focused on building a positive soul, you'll probably find your view of the world is one of abundance. Of course, if you had a more stunted beginning, with parents whose pendulum swung more to the negative, your self view and worldview will be more defeatist.

Thus, the way you feel about yourself (self-esteem) is in direct correlation on how you see yourself (self-image).

Remember, even if you were brought up in a negative household with parents who didn't have the skills or knowledge at the time to empower you, you still have one thing going for you: Choice!

Og Mandino, in his book, The God Memorandum said: "I gave you one more power so great that not even my angels possess it... I gave you the power to choose. With this gift I placed you even above my angels... for angels are not free to choose sin."

In my opinion it is a sin to choose not to live up to your potential. Even if you had shattered childhood, it is past... choose to be a success rather than a failure. Choose to live a life of abundance rather than a life of lack. Choose not to follow the herd into mediocrity.

Learn from this apocryphal story. Two brothers were interviewed. One was a criminal, rotting in jail and the other was a successful, respected pillar of his community. When asked why he had turned out like he had, the brother in jail said: "With a father like mine, what did you expect?" It appears that the father was a total degenerate who had also spent time in jail and when it came to his children, he wouldn't have won a prize in Dad's Weekly. When the successful brother was quizzed as to why he had turned out like he did, his answer was: "With a father like mine, what did you expect?" That's the power of choice.

So, choose to hang out with the high quality people in your life.

Choose to read inspirational books that will light up your path as you make your way through life. Choose an attitude of joy, abundance, appreciation and gratitude rather than one of desolation, despair and disaster. Choose not to let the challenges in life wear you down but rather shine you up like a beautiful diamond.

Choose to believe that you are worthy of having your heart's desire. Because you are.

If you still find this to be a hard sell, choose to start counting your blessings. Have an attitude of gratitude because whatever your situation is now, you still have a lot to be grateful for, don't you?

You have more or less 100-million receptors in our eyes and 24 000 fibres in each ear – at the very least, be grateful for your sight and your hearing.

And, choose to grow. You probably already know that your results will always level out to the degree of your growth. If you don't grow in intellect, skill, self-confidence and stature, you'll keep attracting the same results to yourself.

You don't want success badly enough

Anybody who has read anything by motivational guru, Anthony Robbins will have heard him say that there are only two things that motivate us in life: Avoidance of pain and achievement of pleasure. Most of us are motivated more by the avoidance of pain, aren't we? We make sure we earn enough money so that we can pay our bond each month, pay the kids' school fees and so on. We know that if we lose our job that most of us are one pay cheque away from bankruptcy. This is what I call a fear motivator. We should rather look at pleasure motivation to sustain us. The attitude should be, "If I earn more money, I could have a better lifestyle for me and my family."

Remember, that what you focus on is where your energy will go. Or as psychologist, Carl Jung put it, "What you resist will persist."

If you want to succeed in your life, you have to be prepared to put in the work. If you don't take some kind of action towards your goals, no amount of visualisation and positive thinking is going to make it happen.

Once you've found your purpose and the goals that align to that purpose, you've got to get off your bum. You've got to do the work. You've got to put in the hours because nothing worthwhile ever came easy, did it? Top sports stars have a phenomenal work ethic. Most of them sacrificed a lot to get where they are. Dan Millman, ex-Olympian gymnast said, "Discipline brings excellence and excellence brings freedom."

If you're a student, you've got to put in the work... you have to study to do well. If you're a sales person, you've got to make phone calls every day and see prospects if you want to be a massive success. By working, we create more opportunities for ourselves; we get to pay ourselves more. But, most of us miss out on the opportunity and privilege to work because we don't have a compelling enough purpose and irresistible goals. When our purpose and goals are tepid, I guarantee you we'll be lazy and uninspired. I love what Thomas Edison said about work: "Opportunity is missed by most because it is dressed in overalls and looks like work."

Take the plunge

Make this the crucible moment that you get out of the edge of the rain. Take time to discover why you're here, what it is you really want, believe that you are worthy of success and work hard to get it. If you do that you will have a life of adventure, destiny and purpose. Take the plunge and live the life you were destined to live.

A SAFETY PRESPECTIVE

JÜRGEN TIETZ

Jürgen is a SAFETY expert, professional speaker and author of a book on leadership and life skills. He has 35 years experience in SAFETY, mass production, manufacturing, mining and productivity improvement, plus an authority on communication and people behaviour, especially across cultures. He 'lost' one eye to cancer, was retrenched after 25 years in the explosives industry, is fluent in English, Zulu, Afrikaans and German. Jürgen has been voted as 'Best Ideas' and 'Best Speaker' at International conferences.

He has developed his PEOPLE philosophy and SAFETY gospel - **Systems, Equipment and People, but the most important is People.** MAKING SAFETY SIMPLE is his slogan and he has created electronic toolbox talks and knock-out safety tips, as well as the COOL TOOL™ series of products and handouts. These innovative, unique and unconventional tools and techniques are used to engage those people who make it all happen - the ones **'Who push the buttons and use the tools'.** He is a PARADIGM SHIFTER, using full multi-media presentations and novel hand-outs and techniques to engage the audience and to leave a lasting impression with SAFETY messages that 'stick'.

Tel: (011) 452 0727
Cell: 082 565 8604
jurgen@anda.co.za
www.anda.co.za

A SAFETY PERSPECTIVE

For an engineer, the answer is straight forward: if you want to succeed with any major project or undertaking, you have to plan it well. To take this to the level of a successful (speaking) business, it starts with a business plan. A plan that details your vision and mission, business concept, strategy, resources, financials, risks, rewards and major mile stones. In order to arrive at the overall plan, you have to consider other elements as well - your market, opportunities, competition, key issues facing the market, your approach, key success factors and your USP (unique selling proposition).

Doing a business plan is like laying a foundation. It takes a lot of thinking and you have to get it right as your business will be built on this, even though it is not cast in concrete, can and should change as your business develops, you face new challenges and see new opportunities. The tough part for most people is putting their plan into ACTION – on paper it is of little use!

Apart from taking action, a most important aspect of planning is the review process. You should regularly (six monthly) go back to your business plan and check how you are doing. So often we have wonderful plans, but in the heat of the battle we get sidetracked from our goal. The plan is not an end in itself, but a tool to achieve your vision. The motto is: use it or lose it.

Vision and mission

If you don't know where you are going, chances are that you will end up somewhere else. Focus and determination is absolute key to your business plan. Where do you see yourself and your business next year, within two years, or even in five years time? You want to grow your business – no business is in business to stagnate or to decline. What is your mission, what is your overriding goal, what are you trying to achieve? How will you accomplish this growth of your business? The answer to this question is part of the detailed planning and the road map you have to follow. Below is my own vision and mission:

TO BE THE BEST SAFETY SPEAKER IN AFRICA

These three: Systems, equipment and people – but the greatest of these is people

Market, niche and competition

On what industry, at what level and which aspects of the service (or product) is your focus? This is a most important business decision, as most industries already have too many general practitioners.

My speaking niche has a number of levels. I focus on Safety, not the systems and equipment, but the PEOPLE side of the equation. The next level of PEOPLE is that I target the people 'who push the buttons and use the tools', as well as those who manage them. I talk to senior leadership as well, but I am at my best at the shop floor or rock face. Lately, I concentrate on the Safety representatives, elected by the shop floor to represent safety matters on their behalf to management. A specific need exists at this level and I concentrate on the manufacturing and mining sectors.

A narrow niche helps me to be 'wanted' and, rather than losing business, my business has grown. Working within a narrow niche makes me a specialist in my field and I address and satisfy a very specific requirement which my customers have. I have another benefit: I set myself apart from my competitors. What I do is so unique and focused, with a lot of new and novel ideas, that are difficult for others to clone what I am doing. It helps, of course, that I bring my own style, energy and passion into that niche.

Challenges, threats, key issues and success factors

One of the biggest challenges in any speaking business is, that you are fully accountable. There is no one else, nobody else to blame or to hold responsible. The buck literally stops with you, you are delivering the goods. You are responsible for ensuring a happy client at the end of your presentation. The challenge lies in the fact that you have the freedom to decide what you want to do, how you want to do it, when, where and with whom. You set your own priorities.

The **threat** lies in the fact that the challenges can be intimidating. This pressure may lead to procrastination, especially when faced with unpleasant tasks. For many people, cold call selling is one such task.

A **key issue** for your clients is, that they need an expert. Just being a speaker, engineer, consultant, trainer, coach, facilitator or whatever other professional, is of no value to them. Your value lies in the *manner* in which you deliver your service. Your client is buying, and paying good money, for the distinctive expertise you bring to the party. Make sure your expertise is based on practical experience. The most powerful selling tool is a testimonial – bottom line results which you delivered.

Another key issue is, to ensure that all the support services are taken care of: Even though there is an event organiser, AV technician, venue manager... if they don't deliver, the event will reflect badly on *you* and chances for follow-up business is very slim. Delivery and ACTION is what counts:

There is nothing which moves people more than ACTION and nothing which is more powerful than prompt PRO-ACTIVE ACTION

(Jürgen Tietz)

Do what you say you are going to do, when you say you are going to do it, follow up and follow through to completion. Frustrated clients get put off!

Exceed expectations, deliver more and deliver earlier than promised. Peace of mind is the key!

Business concept and strategy

What makes your business unique? What is your USP – Unique Selling Proposition? If you do not have something unique, novel and of value, then you will be competing, on price only, with everybody else who offers the same as you do. It also helps if your service, style of delivery and products are so unique, that they are difficult to emulate.

I keep shifting the goal post and constantly come up with new products and services, which is the best way to stay ahead of my competition. 'New' does not always mean innovation from scratch, but rather creating unique and novel ways to meet the needs of my customers. I adapt, adopt, and benchmark the best in another industry. I resize, repackage, re-engineer and a host of other re-whatever, as long as it meets my client's needs.

To stay relevant, I am pro-active and change the rules of the game and set the trend in my market niche. However, working at the cutting edge places a burden on my shoulders. I have to be the best I can be, every time, to deliver results which are beyond expectations. I use audience participation and involvement through a customised hand-out.

My novel, unique and flexible **COOL TOOL™** is specifically aimed at *raising awareness* and the need for action. By using a hands-on approach, I get people to "**eKhuluma**" (talk) and take action on a specific topic, be it safety, leadership, change or communication.

My **COOL TOOL™** makes the messages 'stick'. The power of the **COOL TOOL™** lies in its simplicity, in associating everyday items with a specific topic.

The **pillbox** with 5–15 items is customised and branded to my client's specifications. The audience is engaged to link the topic to the pillbox content. This sustains the message and encourages the audience to take the message back to the work place and to their home. Another benefit is, that the delegates will keep and share the pillbox with others, thus sustaining the message. It also makes a smart calling card with my contact details!

I only do what I am best at, the rest I outsource. Locating and using resources which you do not directly employ, is a smart way of doing business. I get results of the highest quality, lowest prices, faster and without the hassles of having to manage employees. I have formed reliable alliances with various individuals who do work for me – from graphic design, desk top publishing, accounting and tax returns, to people who make up and produce many of my customised products. These resources know that their continued business with me depends on how well they deliver. In essence, your clients outsource the speaking / motivation / training / coaching job to you and you better deliver on a sustainable basis, or you are out of a job.

The one resource I am most proud of, and which illustrates the outsourcing concept best, is my Virtual PA. Isabel lives some 2000 km away from where I stay and works from home. I never see Isabel! All our communication is done via email and telephone/cell phone. She does all my support work, all the organising for my speaking events. She does all the things I am not good at, do not enjoy doing or have no passion for. She builds up my data base, runs my group mail system, does invoicing, vendor applications, secures payments, gets testimonials and does many other tasks. She even surfs the internet, looks for business opportunities and has become very pro-active.

At the end of every month she sends me a task break down, time sheet and an invoice for the time spent on my work. I have no idea what she does on a day to day basis, or when she does it. It is none of my concern. What is critical to me, are the results she delivers and the tasks she completes. Isabel knows that, giving me this support on a sustainable basis, is her job security.

The money side of your business

I cannot emphasise this part of the business plan enough, especially if you start from scratch, as a speaker with little or no proven track record. Most small business ventures fold in the first two years, because of a lack in planning the financials.

A good acid test for your business plan is this: can you take your plan to a bank or to a venture capitalist and secure the funds for your business? If the answer is no, then your plan is flawed and it is back to the drawing board for you.

You need to detail how many paid engagements you plan to deliver per year, how much product you will sell and at what price. For me, this was the tough part, because, as the new kid on the block, I had no idea what to charge for my services. I had no products to support my speaking efforts, I had no idea of the cost involved in running a speaking business, I did not understand the tools of the trade, nor did I realise how much I had to invest. I replace my laptop every two years. I have my own back-up AV equipment, remote, digital voice recorder, digital camera, back-up hard drive, printers, scanners and other equipment.

In your business plan you have to allow for the fact that it takes time to find your niche, build up a reputation, build up a data base, find clients, become GOOD at what you do in order to command higher fees and a host of other factors. It took me over three years to achieve this and to get my speaking business off the ground.

Outsource the financial support services – book-keeping and tax returns, unless you are an expert in that field - but keep your eye on your income and expenses! There are no clear cut rules to the money side of this business, because each business model is unique in so many ways. When selling products you need to calculate the real value of programs which you have developed and packaged, books, CD/DVD's and you need to remember that you are selling your intellectual property. Often, it is a lot of work up front, but afterwards the effort is minimal and the profits most handsome.

The business of selling

We are in the business of selling, unless yours is a charity organisation. To many of us, selling is a dirty word, associated with the second-hand-car-salesman image. I used to consider any sales team to be the biggest liability for a company. They always seem to play golf and spend 50% of their time wining and dining with clients. Now that I am running my own speaking business, that paradigm has shifted 180 degrees.

Selling is the toughest part of my business, but it is going out there and getting the job, which puts money in the bank. Selling follows planning and my worth determines my price. To call on a stranger, gain entry, establish trust and respect, form a new relationship, make proposals, overcome objections, deal with rejections, following up again and again and again... and closing out by actually asking for the business!

A key factor with selling is that you have to know and understand your client's needs, as well as the needs of the service sector of your market niche. What does your client expect from a service provider like you? Listen carefully to your clients' needs, but listen to their personal needs as well. What matters to him/her? What will make him/her look good/ succeed? Develop a tool or technique to enable you to read between the lines.

Take at face value what they tell you, but verify this yourself and give feedback. I use my mirror technique to accomplish this. I take photos of the good, the bad and the ugly and then challenge my clients to accept responsibility for what they see in the photos.

I establish personal relationships with my clients. I ask them questions about their background, their origin, their family, and their interests. What makes them tick and what are their likes and dislikes? Sometimes I Google the client's name, look at their company website or search some of the social networks, like Facebook. The amount of information available on the internet is mind boggling. To be able to walk into a 'cold call' meeting and say to Karen: "Is your Beagle, Scruffy, recuperating well from his operation?" knocks the socks off people - they realise that I have come prepared. During the first meeting, I share this kind of information about myself. I have only one eye and use this most effectively to gain entry. Once I have established a personal relationship, selling new products and services to 'old' clients is easy.

A fundamental reason for our reluctance to sell, is our fear of the word 'NO' from the prospective customer. Selling is a business transaction, so I don't take it personally. We often do not 'close' the sale by asking for a commitment. A potential customer may give you one or more of the following reactions to your sales pitch:

- Thanks, but not now/we have to review our strategy.
- I need to check our budget/still decide.
- I need to think about this/will get back to you.
- We have to discuss the options/check with the boss.

I listen for action verbs like think, get, discuss, check, see, decide, review, etc., and then ask: BY WHEN? By when will you get back to me? By when will you make the decision? By when will you check with your boss? This gives me the return ticket for action to be taken by the other person, with a commitment to me. It also makes it very clear that I am serious about closing the sale. I am specific and clear about my intention!

The power of influence

Most of what we say or write is aimed at influencing others. This is especially true if you are standing on the platform in front of an audience. We influence people in many ways, merely by our interaction and presence. Influence is a life skill for speakers. We need the ability to put our ideas into words, listen, understand, persuade and establish a connection. To influence is positive, to manipulate is negative and degrading. Holding the microphone has an element of power, because of the position on the stage. You may have the knowledge and experience, but your audience also holds power: the choice to listen to you. The idea is to get agreement, realisation and understanding by sharing information. This is a 'passive' way of influencing – people have an enormous capacity for, and yearn to absorb information and to use this data to form paradigms. Real power is the capacity to influence, to inspire and to motivate people – creating an environment which allows individuals to *choose* to be fired up and to develop passion.

Influence, trust and respect go hand in hand. You will not heed the message unless you trust the source. The credibility is most often directly associated with the person delivering the message. Be open, be authentic and be worthy of trust and respect. Influence and behaviour go hand in hand. Do not attack an individual's self-esteem. Associate with winners and with people who have a positive influence on you. Build bridges.

Give without expecting to **receive**. Have genuine interest in, and care for other people. Influence and attitude also go hand in hand. Our own self-esteem determines our attitude. This, in turn, rubs off on the people we interact with and sways their reaction to our attempts to influence them. Who wants to follow a loser? Exude confidence! You have a choice – how to behave and react!

Influence and personal interest go hand in hand. People readily commit themselves to things which will further their own agenda. If there is a link between what a person is asked to do and what the person wants to do, then the battle is half won. The trick is to read and understand your audience. Seek to understand first, then to be understood.

Golden rules of influencing

- Be sincere, don't play games, show trust, respect, integrity and build bridges
- Help others get what they want and give without expecting something in return
- Show interest, listen, understand and show genuine care about the well being of others
- Walk your talk, cultivate a positive attitude, exude confidence and take ultra responsibility for your actions

Criteria for a proposal or showcase

It costs time and money to develop a proposal, prepare and attend a sales meeting or do a showcase. That's why I make sure I have a very good chance for success. Here are some questions and guidelines I use to make sure I am not wasting my time: Do I understand the client's problems/issues/needs and expectations thoroughly? Will I provide a satisfactory solution, or even exceed their expectations? The client must experience a current 'pain' or want a significant improvement/ benefit, in order to move or change. Does my proposition/ solution/proposal really add value and can I demonstrate it to the client? Does the client have the necessary resources to solve the problem and is he willing to spend those resources?

If they don't have the money to invest in my solution, I am wasting my time. Do I understand the client's selection criteria? Do I have access to the decision makers/are they attending my showcase? I never make a presentation to someone who can't say 'YES'.

Branding, advertising and websites

When I started my speaking career, I had no focus, no market niche and no brand. I was the typical 'motivational' speaker. I had written a book on leadership and life skills and needed to sell it. I told everybody that I can speak on any topic. You name it, I can do it!

After listening to successful speakers, I realized that I have to establish my expertise and speak about my passion: safety. I chose safety, because safety is in my blood - I worked for an explosives manufacturer for 25 years.

A PR expert worked on my branding. As a result, **eKhuluma** was born and I selected the crocodile as an image for my brand. **COOL TOOL™** became my sub-brand. I spend a lot of time and money on my desk top publishing resource to get the images, colours and the 'look and feel' of my brand.

Having been 'branded', I use **eKhuluma** and **COOL TOOL™** in my speaker's profile, writing, presentations and for advertising. I had product brochures printed and ran advertising campaigns in safety magazines. I branded hand-outs, like key rings, which I freely distributed when meeting with prospects.

I had my 'branded' profile on three websites. As time passed, my 'branding' passion withered away - the branding did not meet my expectations. The phone did not ring off the hook and I was not flooded with enquiries because my name appeared on websites or in adverts.

The unexpected happened. Another sub-brand was created. Many of my audiences referred to me as the **YEBO BABA** guy, because of my audience engagement technique, using these words. I realised that, hiring a speaker is like hiring a band for your daughter's wedding. You have to see and hear them in action, before you are going to commit yourself. To see a wonderful, branded write up or snazzy website is not going to put your mind at ease. A testimonial, referral or video clip will help, but it does not beat seeing the real McCoy in action. This is why I find showcases an effective marketing tool.

I no longer advertise, nor do I spend time or money on websites and social media. I put all my energy into doing demos in my market niche of manufacturing, mining, and safety events. Isabel contacts associations, institutes, councils, federations and societies which operate in my market niche with three targeted questions: when is your next event, who organises it and are you using speakers at your event? Depending on the type of association and size of the event, it sometimes ends up as a paid engagement with the organisers buying my hand-outs.

Tools, tips, techniques and tactics

Below are a number of ideas, tips and tricks I have picked up over the years through own insight or from the many speakers I have seen in action:

- Develop a list of '10 questions' to put to a prospect - requirements, expectations, size of the opportunity, who will make the buying decision, as well as the amount of money available.
- It is best to sell to a group, or team of people. Top of the range is the EXCO. This way you establish rapport with more than one person. When people move position, or resign, you still have support in the company.
- Make sure your tools of the trade are top of the range. You should have your own back-up AV equipment, remote, DVR, digital camera, etc.
- Your voice is your number one tool. Go for voice training. Learn how to care for, and use, your voice more effectively. Learn how to warm up your voice before taking to the stage.

- Find tools and techniques to put into your offering. You need to 'give your talk legs'.

- Always allow enough time to arrive at the venue early, to settle down and to make sure everything is in working order. For big events, I often arrive the day before and sleep over. This gives me plenty of time to check out the venue, test the AV equipment, listen to what the other speakers have to say and focus on my own presentation.

- Always ask for a testimonial. Apart from being a powerful tool for selling yourself, added as an attachment to proposals, it validates your client's appreciation for your service or product. It often also opens the door for follow-up business.

- Listen to your clients – it will give you the ammunition and inspiration to develop new tools, techniques and products. More products in your arsenal mean opportunities for follow-ups, instead of a once-off engagement.

- Write regularly – A column for a magazine, or your own newsletter. This has two benefits: It will help you sharpen your saw to build your expertise and you will become known as an expert in your niche.

- Build up a database to use as a mailing list for your newsletter. I send out Safety Tips to some 2000 people every fortnight. I offer free advice and relevant safety information on the current Safety Tip. I include a hook, by offering something additional. I then follow up on the opportunity this generates.

- Find ways of engaging the audience in your talk or presentation. Use a non-threatening technique. Audience engagement has a powerful impact and often provides a lot of humour. The risk with this technique is that you may sacrifice control over content and time of your presentation.
- Take photos of relevant things and situations and link it in the right context, preferably with some humour.

Insights, lessons and points of wisdom

1. **No Sales** equals **no business**. Period!
2. First you need to become **GOOD**. All else follows. If you are GOOD, you will leave with the follow-up, or with the next opportunity, already in the pipeline.
3. Build a mutual relationship, also with other speakers. **GIVE** without wanting to **GET**, especially money! Share advice and knowledge and help freely. When I hear of clients moving to a new job, or company, I send them my 'New job checklist' and offer to coach them in their new role - free of charge.
4. Be authentic, tell your own stories and have FUN. You have to enjoy what you are doing, otherwise how can you expect anyone else to have fun?
5. The audience is on your side. They have come to listen to, and learn from *you*. They want you to succeed.
6. True speaking is not a contest. It's not about you, what you have, know or want. It's about the needs of your audience - how can you help them?
7. Very few experts have a truly radical and novel concept, which would warrant starting afresh. We need to understand that our clients have been at their business for years. We should empower them to deliver better results, faster. We should enhance their existing systems and processes.

8. If the audience departs not talking your talk, you did not engage them. They are your best sales force! Create memory hooks and handouts to sustain the impact.
9. People are tired of manuals, papers and posters – it is such a waste of paper and will be used for 'shelf development' only! Look for, and develop, something new, something fresh, with a longer shelf life.
10. Less is more. Focus and find your niche, it will increase your business.
11. Your business will, and should, change over time. It indicates growth – hopefully not only in volume, but growth in your product and services portfolio as well. Products and services have a life cycle and something that worked well five years ago, is outdated today. This holds especially true, if you want to be the leader in your field of expertise.
12. The gestation period in the speaking business is long. You need financial reserves, hard work, excellence and patience to make it to the top.
13. You need **PASSION** for the niche you have chosen. This passion has to shine through and be contagious to your audience.
14. Ron Arden is coach to international speakers. He defines the purpose of speaking as follows: *To research, package and deliver information, by providing a fresh insight and a few points of wisdom, in such a manner as to influence the thinking of an audience and move them into action.* Your audience needs to leave your presentation thinking differently about your topic. If they don't, no action will result and you will have wasted your and their time.
15. I have many failures. This is part of the game, because I constantly push the envelope.

A SIMPLE SUCCESS SYSTEM

RICHARD MULVEY

Richard Mulvey is South Africa's leading seminar speaker and over the last 16 years has inspired and motivated over 140,000 business people throughout Europe, Asia and Africa. Richard's impressive client list includes most of South Africa's leading corporate companies.

Richard is the past President of the Professional Speakers' Association of Southern Africa and a member of the Global Speakers Federation.

Richard is a prolific writer and has published 17 books, as well as over 50 DVDs, CDs and MP3s all available worldwide through Amazon.com.

Apart from a successful corporate career Richard has also worked for the Queen in Buckingham Palace, written and marketed a multi-restaurant accounting package called "Trade Inn". Travelled overland from London to South Africa and back again and recently climbed Kilimanjaro to raise R70,000 for Reach for a Dream. Richard's passion is moving minds and creating understanding where there was just confusion and he is the perfect Sales Motivator for your next convention.

> Tel: 0861 444 888/+27 31 563 5316
> Cell: 083 280 9800
> richard@richardmulvey.com
> www.richardmulvey.com

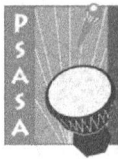 # A SIMPLE SUCCESS SYSTEM

In 1996, I started to write a book about being successful. I had just completed my first book "Presenting for Profit" and that was slow to get off the mark. My business had been in existence for two years and like many start-ups in the first few years I was not yet making a profit, least not that you would notice. I was still driving an 8 year old Audi 400 that had experienced more than 300,000 kilometres of our wonderful countryside first hand and I was selling myself as a success guru.

When I was asked to speak to local corporate businesses I would park my car some distance from the offices in the hope that my host would not feel inclined to walk me to the car. I am not saying it was tough, I don't remember it like that at all. I remember it as exciting, exhilarating, risky for sure, but every contract secured made a huge difference and warranted a huge celebration. I remember on more than one occasion spending more on the celebration than the contract would make. I guess we needed it.

What then possessed me to write a guide to success you may ask, from a position that most people would consider to be a lack of success.

This is an interesting question, but you know, I never considered myself to be unsuccessful, even in those early days. I always knew what I was doing was working. I always knew that I would make a go of it. I always knew how to be successful. We all do. Despite the name of this book, there is, in fact, no secret to being successful. Deep down you know how to be successful so my small contribution to this book is just reminding you of what you already know.

You are making a choice. You are choosing whether to be successful or not. Today, right now, you are making a conscious choice whether to make a success of your life or not. Most people decide upon the latter rather than the former which is good news for you. There is a thousand times more competition amongst those people who choose not to be successful than those people who have made a conscious choice to be successful. Success is easier than failure.

I finished writing the book in 1997 and there is no doubt that it was a labour of love. It was really my third book ("You've only got 4 minutes" had been published in the meantime) but it was the one I was most proud of and when I developed the series of pocket guides that are the mainstay of my published work I called it number one. All that was 14 years ago now and the world and I have moved on together, the principles that create success in a corporate environment, however, have never changed.

There is no secret to being successful. The process of being successful has been long known and well documented for centuries. From today's great motivational thinkers like Stephen Covey, Anthony Robbins, John Kehoe, Dale Carnegie, Suze Orman to the great philosophers going back over thousands of years. If you read what all these great men and women have to say the first thing you will discover is they are all saying pretty much the same thing. There is no secret.

In fact, the principles that I will discuss over the next few pages are in your brain already you just need to bring them to the surface and act upon them to be successful.

To make the process easy to understand, I have narrowed it down into one sentence. One simple sentence that, if followed, will guarantee that you will achieve whatever you want at work.

The Simple Success System

Take control of your life, plan what you want to achieve and focus upon it, decide to make a change and take action.

Simple, isn't it!

Well, it is simple but the sentence does not really do justice to the system. There are five key words or phrases in the sentence and we will take them one at a time to explore their real meaning.

Take Control　Plan　Focus
Decide　Action

Take Control of your life

Who is in control of your life?

I have asked that question of many thousands of people over the years and I get many different answers. The most common seem to be "Are you kidding? My wife of course!" or "My boss is in control", or "Well, at the moment my young children seem to be in control".

You may be thinking "Well, I am in control of my life", but are you? Do you take responsibility for the way in which everything affects you? If not, you are in trouble already.

Sure it's easy to be responsible for the daily stuff like getting up, going to work, to buy flowers for your wife, or a little something for your husband. But what about the things you apparently have no control over, do you take responsibility for the way they affect you? Most people draw the line there. In fact most people draw the line much closer to home because it is easier to become a victim than to take responsibility.

What do I mean by "Victim"?

There is a little of the victim in all of us. A victim would rather find someone or something to blame than find a solution. You will hear two or three victim statements every day at work and you will sometimes catch yourself being a victim. Consider the following:

- *"I am late this morning because the bus was early and I missed it."*
- It's the bus's fault.
- *"My report is late because the printer was broken."*
- It's the printer's fault.

By blaming somebody or something else for the situation you are in, you can sit back in the comfortable knowledge that it's somebody else's responsibility to fix. The problem arises when you discover that by making it somebody else's responsibility you are giving away your ability to respond. (response - ability). By blaming the printer, what you are actually saying is that your life is controlled by a printer. This is not good!

You may be thinking that it doesn't matter what we say as long as we can fix it, but in fact, it does matter. What you are saying right now has a fundamental effect on your destiny. The way it works is like this:

What you say regularly, has a controlling interest over what you do.

This is obvious. We all know that if we say things over and over again we convince ourselves that they are true and we act upon that truth.

What you do regularly becomes a habit.

Your habits control your destiny.

We have to take back control of the words we use because they are controlling our destiny.

To fix this problem you first need to take back responsibility.

For instance:

- *"My report was late because I was cutting it too fine."*
- *It's my Fault!*

This is tough of course. It's far easier to blame others than to take responsibility. But if you take responsibility (the ability to respond) for everything that happens in your life, you can empower yourself to make things work for you. You can change your status from a victim to a winner simply by adding action to the statement.

For Instance:

- *"My report was late because I was cutting it too fine but next month I will do it a day earlier and can then print it on any printer so my report will never be late again."*
- *It's my fault but I've fixed it!*

Finally to be a real winner you must take advantage of that wonderful word that losers talk about and winners act upon.

"Pro-activity"

Winners will be looking ahead proactively to avoid potential victim situations by fixing them in advance.

For instance:

- *"I knew the printer was playing up so I wrote my report a day earlier just in case there was a problem."*
- *I fixed it in advance!*

If you don't take control of the way in which everything affects you, you become a victim and victims simply "go with the flow" without direction and without achieving anything very much.

Start the day by saying "I am the only person who is responsible for what happens to me" and turn victim situations into winning solutions.*"*

Plan what you want to achieve

Do you have a written plan for your life? In my experience about 3% of the people I ask this question say "yes", but these are usually the most successful 3%!

I know what you are thinking. You are thinking that you know exactly what you want to achieve in your life and it is all in your head. That's fine of course except there is no commitment to a thought pattern. Ever wondered what happened to those wonderful ideas that you had last year, what you were going to do, the successes you were going to achieve. It is very difficult to put ideas into action until they are written down.

Think about your company strategy for this year. Can you imagine what would have happened during the year if the strategy had not been in writing? That's right, nothing!

To start to build your corporate life to achieve your full potential you need to have a clear picture of what you want to achieve in your mind. You need to visualise the finished product before you start to put the pieces together.

Take some time to imagine what you would like to achieve in your corporate life. Make some notes now. There will be plenty of time later to polish it up and get it right so just let your mind go. Dream a little and write down the results.

Now we come to the first obstacle! It has been pretty easy so far but we need to get beyond a blockage that 95% of the people in the world never get beyond.

Many years ago, when I was a young man, I attended a session with one of the motivational speakers of the day and he talked to us about writing down our goals. "When you write down your goals" he said "make sure they are realistic goals. If you write down unrealistic goals they will be so far away that you can't imagine yourself getting there. You can't visualise them so you probably won't achieve them."

I thought about this for a while and it occurred to me that if everybody wrote down realistic goals where do the truly great people come from? Surely in order to achieve greatness some people must have written down unrealistic goals?

When you are writing down your goals make sure you are writing unrealistic goals. Realistic is a code word for low but there is the problem.

Do you believe you could earn a million over the next twelve months?

No? Why not?

Plenty of people earn that sort of money, so why not you?

No, I am not joking. The problem is not the money, the problem is in your belief system. You believe you are not able to earn that much money so you don't.

We all have a belief system that is designed to protect us but in fact, it is holding us back. Your belief system has been built up over many years from many different sources but as far as you are concerned your belief system is absolute fact.

Teachers have a lot to do with the way in which belief systems are developed. "Sorry little Johnny" says the teacher "You will never be an artist. You may be an accountant one day but you will never be an artist". So Johnny doesn't try to be an artist.

He goes through his life with the same belief and at 75 years old he looks back at his life and says "You know, my teacher was absolutely right, I never became an artist". Well, of course he never became an artist, he didn't try to become an artist.

So what is in your belief system that is holding you back?
Many years ago when I had just left school I was at a loose end wondering what I should do with my life. I wasn't a great academic achiever and had always had problems with my spelling. The result of that was that I wrote badly hoping that a scribble would hide incorrectly spelt words and the result of that was nobody knew what on earth I was writing about. Being a young man without any career mapped out for me, my Mother said to my Father "Why don't you take Richard into the business with you?"

"What!" said my Father "Richard? In my business? What's he going to do? He can't write, he can't spell, what's he going to do in my business?"

So I am listening to this conversation and there is a man I respect telling me that I can't write so that goes into my belief system.

I didn't write my first book until I was 45 years old.

You see, I had to get beyond my belief system before I could write. Since then, of course, I have been very prolific with my writing. Once I had taken that particular belief and questioned it the floodgates opened and I have, as I write, published 16 books and many articles and other publications. If I trusted my belief system I would still be back there bubbling with ideas but bookless.

I ask you again. What is in your belief system that is holding you back? We have already discovered that you don't believe that you can earn a million over the next 12 months, so what else is in there that you haven't questioned recently?

Would you like a greater salary than you have at the moment? Maybe you are thinking that you wouldn't know what to do with all that extra cash but for most people a greater salary is very attractive. If you are one of these people, I have some news for you. You are earning, at this moment, precisely what you believe you should be earning, no more and no less. Your belief system is telling you what you are worth and that is what you strive for.

I employed a salesman some years ago by the name of William. William was a great guy and had the personality to be a great salesman although he had yet to prove that. I was very impressed with his skills however, and after a period of developing product knowledge and improving his skills I had a space in a very good area and rather than promoting someone else to that area I slipped William straight in. The previous salesperson in that area did reasonably well and brought in 180,000 in commission during the year but I expected William to do better.

At the end of William's first year selling in the area his results were disappointing earning for himself only 60,000 commission, so I had no choice but to move him out. You may think that is tough but that is selling. You can easily see if a person is performing and if they don't they have to go. The problem is that I really liked William and I didn't want to get rid of him so I moved him into a really bad area in the hope that he would see the light and resign.

William was not happy with the move but he understood the situation and promised to make a go of this bad area. He got stuck in and the results were amazing. I had not even covered this area in the past because the commission possible in the area would only amount to about 30,000 but William really worked hard and managed to increase the business in the area to earn 60,000 in commission.

I was delighted of course and told people that I had justified my faith in the salesman so I promoted him to a much better area so that he could apply his new found enthusiasm and earn more. What do you think he earned in the third year?

You guessed it, 60 thousand.
William was a 60 thousand a year man. That is what his belief system told him he should earn so that is what he worked towards.

When you write down your goals you need to make sure that you think beyond your belief system. Set yourself unrealistic goals. Don't worry just yet how you are going to achieve them, for the moment just dream them and write them down.

Dream it.   Write it down.   Dream it.

So, let's think of an unrealistic goal to focus on. How about taking over from my mate Bill? You know Bill... He runs a fairly successful computer company in the States. Bill Gates that is, the richest man in the world. Do you think that is unrealistic enough? I'd say!

Before you finish this book you will realise that you could go for that if you want to. Trust me for the time being.

When you write down your goals you must write them as if you have already achieved them. "I am President of Microsoft" or "I have achieved sales person of the year this year" If that's what you want.

Now Date it!

Once you have written down what you want to achieve you need to date stamp it. There is no commitment until you have written next to it the date you want to achieve it by. A plan without a date is a wish list.

Now let's make that unrealistic goal more realistic

The reason why the goal we have set for ourselves (President of Microsoft... remember?) is so unrealistic is it seems so far away, it is unobtainable in just one lifetime. To make it more realistic we need to break it down into things that we can do rather than things that we cannot.

There is a process that I have discussed in my book on decision making called "Future Perfect decisions" and we can use the same principle in this process as well. Future perfect decisions forces you to put yourself in the result of the decision and ask yourself how you got there. You look down the time line and see each step as if you have taken it already. Then simply go back and take each step in turn.

For instance:

Put yourself in the position of President of Microsoft, and ask yourself "How did I get here?" Well, before I was President of Microsoft I must have been Vice President for a while" So take one step back. Now you are Vice President of Microsoft how did you get there? "Before I was Vice President I must have worked for Microsoft in America for at least ten years" So take one step back.

"Now I am working for Microsoft in America, how did I get here?" Before I worked for Microsoft in America I probably worked for Microsoft in this country, so take one step back. "Now I am working for Microsoft in this country, how did I get here?"

"Before I worked for Microsoft, I must have had the qualifications, so take one step back and I am doing a degree in Computer Engineering, how did I get there?"

"Before I started on my degree I must have applied to do a correspondence course or to the local university."

"But wait a minute! That's where I am now, and in order to be President of Microsoft all I have to do today is to write one letter."

Once you have written that letter it is not a wild stretch of the imagination to believe that you will be accepted to do that degree course. And if you put your mind to it there is no reason at all why you shouldn't get that degree. Once you have a degree in Computer Engineering and if you want to enough, you can apply to work for Microsoft etc... etc....

You see greatness was never achieved in a single step. When I talked about taking over Microsoft as a target you thought to yourself that was a wild, unrealistic target because you could not imagine yourself as you are now, in that position. But of course, if you get in that position you would not be as you are now.

Greatness is never achieved in a single step. Greatness is always achieved in a million little steps. If you want to be awarded as the greatest salesperson of the year this year then imagine yourself winning the award at the end of the year and ask yourself how you got there. Look back down the time line and see the steps you took, then reverse the process and take those steps. Simple!

We all have greatness in us. Few of us realise our potential because we underrate ourselves. We set realistic targets and just scrape by. We need to set unrealistic targets if we are truly going to start to tap into our potential, then break down that unrealistic target into "Do-able" chunks. Start to work on the things you can do now and you will realise that that unrealistic target gets closer and more realistic as you progress.

Focus

All the great 'success' authors agree: "You get what you focus on".

If you play golf you will have your own examples of how this works. Every time you play the course there will be one hole that always trips you up. It may be the 16th or the 17th and each time you tee off you go straight into the wood or the water trap. You know this, so the next time you are at the 16th, with your best customer behind you watching, you think to yourself "Please Lord, not into the wood again, anywhere else but not into the wood". So you are focussed on the wood, guess where the ball goes!

This is a new twist to Murphy's Law and might perhaps be called Mulvey's Law.

"You always get what you don't want if you focus on not getting it."

Of course the reverse of this is also true and much more important for us if we are going to be successful in our corporate life.

"You always get what you want if you focus on getting it."

When you play golf you know not to focus on avoiding the water trap, but to see yourself driving straight down the fairway.

In the corporate environment it is exactly the same. Every morning when you get to work spend 10 minutes focusing on what you want to achieve. Get out your written plan and visualise what it will be like having achieved those things. Now when you make decisions during the day they will be based upon your morning visualisation and each decision will take you one little step further towards your goals.

Decide to make a Change

We are not good at making decisions. Why?... Because we don't like getting things wrong. The problem is that mistakes are a fundamental part of any success story.

It is not the decisions you get right that matter so much, it is the decisions you get wrong that will more often point to the best steps towards a successful future.

Today's good decisions are based upon yesterday's experiences. Yesterday's experiences are based as much upon your failures as upon your successes.

Nobody in business is a success without being a failure first. It is not possible. Anybody who breaks new ground with their decisions knows that a good number of them will not work.

So now is a good time to start. Take a decision to focus on your goals. Ask yourself, "What decisions would I make today if I knew I could not fail?" Write it down.

Okay. Now apart from the possibility of making a mistake, what else is holding you back?

Winners know that mistakes are an essential part of the process. So do it! Write down what you are going to do **today** that will progress you towards your success in your corporate environment.

Take Action

For some people this is the hardest part. The planning, the focusing, the deciding, they are all easy, but there comes a point when you are standing on the brink and you have to take that step. When you decide of course, there should be no room for hesitation. Decisions are not wishes, they arc carved in stone but sometimes they are put off and get harder and harder to action.

I have a personal rule that I borrowed from Anthony Robins... you can have it if you like! "Never leave the place of a decision without taking some action towards the completion of that decision." This simple rule, if applied, will make a huge difference to the way you make decisions work for you.

So, the moment you take a decision your should take action to cement the decision in place.

And that's it! It's that simple!

Take control of your life, plan what you want to achieve and focus upon it, decide to make a change and take action.

Thank you for taking the time to work through this simple success system with me, I hope you took part in the process rather than just being a spectator.

I estimate that I am probably about halfway through my life and yet I have had far more wonderful experiences and challenges than most people fit into two or three lifetimes. I have been fortunate of course, there have been a number of life threatening situations that could have easily gone either way, but they worked out, most things do.

If you want to make a change in your life, achieve the unachievable, then you will have to take a few risks. The alternative is to look back on missed opportunities, and that makes no sense at all.

In the end it all comes down to one decision; one moment in time; one press of the button; or signature on a piece of paper. You can analyse it to death of course, or you can take Nike's advice and...

Just do it!

HOW CAN YOU THRIVE[3]
while others are barely surviving?

SHARON KING

Sharon King is a **dynamic communicator** with over 14 years experience in the field of adult education and corporate facilitation. She is currently the **Vice President of the Johannesburg Chapter of the Professional Speakers Association of South Africa** (PSASA) and a registered **Education, Training and Development Practitioner** (ETDP).

Sharon also practices as a **Life Coach** and **Neuro-Linguistic Programming** (NLP) **Practitioner** at a **masters level**. To ensure that she can offer you the very best – and varied – support, Sharon engages in continual self-development and learning and is currently completing her psychology degree.Key Steps consulting and training interventions are results driven. It's Sharon's vision and commitment to empower others to reach their potential, motivate themselves, and focus on organisational goals and market objectives through team work and communication. Her passion for life and learning and belief that you are inherently capable of achieving anything you choose to will **inspire you to realise just how brilliant, talented and magnificent you really are**. Sharon works hand-in-hand with organisations – positioning them for long-term success.

Tel: (011) 616 9712
Cell: 082 330 1558
sharon@keysteps.co.za
www.keysteps.co.za

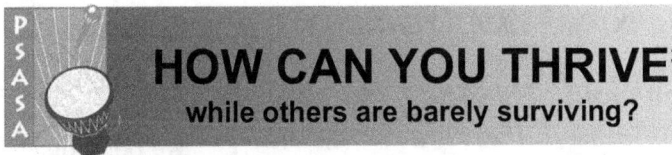

HOW CAN YOU THRIVE³
while others are barely surviving?

> **"No pressure, no diamonds".**
> Mary Case

Are there really any 'secrets' to success left out there? You are probably saying, no and you'd be right. What is often referred to as a 'secret' is really just age old wisdom we have either lost, forgotten to apply or failed to modernise to work in our current corporate environment. So let's get to work and see how easy it can be for you to **THRIVE³** under today's corporate pressures and stresses and create success YOUR WAY.

THRIVE³ is a tool created from years of researching my own and other successful people's strategies; it's filled with wisdom I *really do apply every day* and not just designed to be another theoretical list of helpful hints.

> **"Talk does not cook rice."**
> Chinese Proverb

You'll see that each aspect of **THRIVE³** has three essential practical components (aka 'secrets'). While you are reading and exploring with me, please pick up your pen (or use a highlighter) and identify the main Key Steps you will start taking right now to **THRIVE³** and...

'be the difference that makes the ***difference***'

T^3 *(THINKING - TIME - TENACITY)*

1. Watch your *THINKING*, it really does affect your reality: Always be positive. ***Thoughts about success breed success,*** the same way thoughts about failure often breed failure.

> "What we think, we become."
> Buddha

I am not talking 'rah rah' positivity here. There will be times when you'll get emotionally low or feel discouraged, we all do and we actually need 'down' to recognise when we are 'up'. The key is to acknowledge your feelings, learn the lesson(s), dust yourself off and take positive action. Successful people thrive on successful thoughts. And we all know that our thoughts create our words and our words create our actions. Just think about what happens to the person who thinks that they get flu every winter? Yip, they do, don't they? ***What thoughts are you thinking today? They will affect your actions tomorrow!***

2. Treat your *TIME* as the non-renewable resource it is: When you waste time surfing the Internet, standing in a second

> "It has been my observation that most people get ahead during the time that others waste."
> Henry Ford

long queue because you forgot some important item on your grocery list or left your errands to the last minute and have no choice but to wait, how much does it cost you? Do you know how much an hour of your time is worth? Although we cannot equate everything to a monetary value (some moments are priceless) you can start by taking your monthly salary and dividing it by the number of hours you work a month (about 176 hours).

Once time is gone, it's gone forever and you cannot manufacture any more of it. You can, however, choose how you use it. Take stock of your common time wasters (unnecessary meetings, getting stuck in traffic, working at the wrong time, etc.) and plug the holes that drain your time and energy. You need every bit you have to focus on your work and personal goals.

3. Be *TENACIOUS*: The corporate world is not for sissies! You need to be determined, driven and tenacious about achieving the success you dream of. How many times do you think Colonel Sanders (who eventually created the legendary franchise, KFC) heard no before he got the answer he wanted? He was refused 1009 times before he got his first yes! He spent 2 years driving across America in his beat up car, sleeping in the back seat in his rumpled white suit, eager to get up each day to share his idea with someone. How many people do you think would go through 1009 "no's" before getting their first "yes"?

If you look at any of the most successful people in history, you will find this common thread. ***They would not allow anything to deter them from making their vision a reality.*** Walt Disney was refused financing 302 times before he got the funds to create his

> "Be like a postage stamp; stick to it until you get there."
> Bob Proctor

dream. He was a visionary and more importantly, committed to making that vision a reality; just like Colonel Sanders. Persistence pays. Remember that...

Success is a marathon, not a sprint.

H^3 *(HOPE - HONESTY - HELP)*

1. Never lose your ability to *HOPE*: Studies (such as the one conducted by the telecoms group O2) show how important ***obsessive optimism*** is for ***overall success***. Being hopeful fuels tenacity and your ability to think, talk and behave more positively. Never underestimate its power. While it's

> **"Optimism is the faith that leads to achievement. Nothing can be done without hope and confidence."**
> Helen Keller

true that some of us are predisposed to optimism (i.e. we are born that way), ***being optimistic is something you can learn*** and here's a good place to start... Think about three things when you explain events – PERMANENCE, PERVASIVENESS and PERSONALISATION.

When you are explaining positive events, you want them to be permanent, universal and internal. For example, "All the good things (universal) that happen in my life are always (permanent) a result of my hard work and determination (internal)." When you are explaining negative events, you want them to be temporary, specific and external. For example, "The flat tyre I had today (specific) was the result of some nails that were spilled on the highway (external and temporary)." Contrast that with, "I always (permanent) get flat tyres because I (internal) can never (permanent) avoid all road hazards out there." It's up to you. ***Choose to be optimistic!***

2. Practice *HONESTY*: Remember that ***the first person you need to honest with is yourself***. What do you truly want? What is important to you? Are you taking steps to create the life you dream? Are you being real with yourself about your strengths and weaknesses?

> **"Be who you are and say what you feel, because those who mind don't matter and those who matter don't mind."**
> Dr Seuss

Being honest often requires the ability to *say no so that you can make your yeses matter.* If you find saying "no" a challenge, remember not to confuse rejecting a request with rejecting the person making the request. Saying "no" doesn't mean you don't like the person, just that you're refusing their current request, and vice versa. Also keep in mind that people are usually happier to accept an honest "no", than be faced with indecision and a delayed refusal. Start being truly honest with yourself and others today. *No hiding or ostrich behaviour! It'll only hurt your own success in the long run.*

3. **Ask for *HELP:*** Success is a team sport. I learnt what all the greats before me have known the hard way... **that I cannot do everything on my own.** There are two main reasons for this: firstly, I am actually not good at everything (our egos all need to really get this lesson; I was a bit put out at first but then actually quite relieved I couldn't do it all) and secondly, I just don't have the energy for it all.

> **"Ask, and ye shall receive; seek, and ye shall find; knock, and it shall be opened."**
> Bible

While it is important to have knowledge, skills and experience in your field (success isn't an accident), it is equally important to *hire the right people and learn how to delegate.* You can start today by implementing the **'SMARTER'** strategy... to delegate effectively, tasks must be: **SPECIFIC, MEASURABLE, ACTION-ORIENTATED, REALISTIC, TIME CONSTRAINED** (and if you find letting go of the reins a challenge, set the deadline a little earlier than really necessary to give you peace of mind), **ETHICAL** and **RECORDED.**

R^3 *(RAPPORT & RELATIONSHIPS - RULES - RESULTS)*

1. Build *RAPPORT* and nurture *RELATIONSHIPS*: All the technical expertise in the world won't help if people don't want to work with you. In any aspect of life, success depends on your ability to understand and

> **"Seek first to understand, then to be understood."**
> Stephen R Covey

establish relationships. Remember, *to build rapport you don't have to like or agree with the other person's map of the world*, but you have to at least understand it.

The co-developers in the field of Neuro Linguistic Programming (NLP) began studying people who had the ability to develop rapport quickly with others in client/patient environments, family relationships, sales situations and other contexts. Since then, thousands of people all over the world are benefiting by the simple applications of rapport techniques.

Take a few moments each day to master and use the following techniques and suddenly you will see, hear and feel a profound difference in the way people respond to you. You can use them when making a sale, on a first date, when talking to your teenager, when dealing with your boss or employee and especially when you want to 'get through' to someone you are having a challenge dealing with.

Match the other person's non-verbal behaviour. Stand like them, walk like them and sit like them. Notice how they move and remain still. Adopt your posture so that it is a match or mirror image of theirs. Do the same with the gestures they use. If they fold their arms and lean back or if they cross their legs, you do it too. Match their voice. If they speak in hushed tones or in loud tones, do the same. If they speak fast or slow, you can speed up or slow down and so on.

Subtlety is the key. Do this discreetly. If you follow them too quickly it may appear as if you are mimicking them. You want the matching and mirroring to remain outside their conscious awareness. The trick here is not to be thinking about 'mimicking' them but rather adopt a mindset of getting into their map of the world and developing a relationship.

After a few moments of matching and mirroring, gently begin to use the voice tone and posture which is comfortable for you. When you have established rapport, the other person will begin to follow your movements. ***Rapport is like a dance*** where one leads and the other follows. If the person has picked up your lead, you know you are on your way to establishing a good connection. If not, match until they follow your lead.

It's also important, especially with people you do not naturally connect with, to ***find the 1% you have in common and give it 99% of your attention***. Find common ground and a point of connection as quickly as possible to avoid alienating others. That doesn't mean you have to become friends with and like everyone. In fact, it might be important to break rapport with certain individuals who are negative, energy draining and unsupportive. ***When building relationships, be careful who you associate yourself with as we are often judged by the company we keep.*** You might think it shouldn't matter but it does! Choose your relationships wisely.

2. Know the RULES: *You can't play the game if you don't know the rules.* We all know that companies have unwritten rules. It pays to understand yours. In fact, *it's like being street smart* and if

> **"After the game, the king and the pawn go into the same box."**
> Italian proverb

you analysed successful CEOs, you'd notice that they have an intuitive grasp of the unwritten rules of their organisation.

Where do the unwritten rules actually come from? Various factors contribute, including national and local culture, the economic climate, regulations, people's private agendas and the perceived behaviour of top managers. Here's an example: there could be a written rule that says, "To become a top manager, you need broad experience," but the unwritten rule says, "To get to the top, job-hop as fast as possible." Or a written rule that says, "Managers are accountable for their P&Ls," that gets interpreted as, (1) "Protect your own turf and look after number one" (because there's no reward from growing someone else's empire) and (2) "Watch your quarterlies". In a scenario like this, teamwork might be held as a top organisational value but when written rules get transmuted, teamwork goes out the window.

You can't get to the top without understanding unwritten rules. *Pay attention and become street smart in order to thrive.*

3. Drive for RESULTS: *People want to back a winner and be part of a winning team.* I saw this dynamic at play at the World Cup 2010 final. Many of the Dutch supporters took off their orange wigs and put their scarves and hats into their bag when their team lost and Spain went home with the trophy. Are you disappointed? Yes? So was I. But it was a good reminder that this is part of the reality I live in and the way people often act.

People want to win and get discouraged when they don't achieve results. Keep your focus on where you want to go and how you are going to get there.

Sometimes, in order to get results you have to be prepared to confront non-performance. And sometimes even remove the non-performers if they don't want to shape-up. Being successful isn't about always being the 'Mr Nice Guy'. ***Make sure that you are tough on poor results and***

> **"If you always do what you've always done, you'll always get was you've always got."**
> Henry Ford

easy on the person. By that I do not mean going soft or ignoring non-performance (that just makes performance standards a joke); I mean learning some skills for handling situations more effectively and inspiring change.

Let me give you an example; I often hear people talking about "problem colleagues" or "difficult customers". Firstly, let's stop referring to them as difficult people or problematic because that makes it sound like they have a personal defect and there's not much we can do about that. Refer instead to the precise behaviours that create the difficulty or the problem. For example, rather than saying "she's too talkative" (an adjective which implies something about her personality) say instead, "she talks too much which distracts others in the team" (this describes a behaviour that you can therefore tackle). Or if someone is not telling you the whole truth, avoid saying "he's a liar", rather say, "he is not telling me the whole truth".

Use behaviour words rather than personality or identity words. Then when you approach the person who is causing difficulty, you can tackle their behaviour (which can be changed) rather than their identity (which can't be changed).

I^3 *(INVOLVE - INGENUITY - INTEGRITY)*

1. *INVOLVE* people: When you build rapport and get people involved, they are more likely to co-operate and work as a team. They will also be more committed to solving problems and achieving goals. This success factor is critical in our personal and professional lives.

> "At the end of it all, the most overwhelming key to a child's success is the positive involvement of parents."
> Jane D. Hull

Another trait of successful people is their ability to *focus on people's strengths and catch people doing things right*. Our culture is obsessed with focusing on negative behaviour. We do it with our families at home and in the workplace. Strangely, it seems that criticising and negative thinking are now considered "realistic". While support, praise and encouragement are often considered insincere or manipulative. Let's shift that culture right now and catch at least three people doing things RIGHT in the next 24 hours. Then let's keep the habit going until it just become part of our daily routine to empower and motivate others. Great leaders use this skill to make the world a better place and *achieve the levels of success that separate the 'good' from the 'great'*.

2. Be *INGENIOUS*: Don't be afraid to innovate. ***Dare to be different***. Following the herd is a sure way to mediocrity. Become known as the person who says "Can't is not an option" and then follow through with an 'out-the-box' idea. Ask yourself, ***"What would I do if I wasn't afraid?"*** And

> "Never tell people how to do things. Tell them what to do and they will surprise you with their ingenuity."
> George S. Patton

you might make a mistake; but ***I call mistakes 'magnificent miracles'*** because that's exactly what they are when we are open to getting the lesson they can teach us.

3. Display the highest *INTEGRITY*: Managers are always striving to do things right. Successful leaders, on the other hand, are intent on doing the right thing. Because they know that ***if you don't have personal integrity, you have nothing.***

> "Real integrity is doing the right thing, knowing that nobody's going to know whether you did it or not."
> Oprah Winfrey

Integrity in leadership is expressed in terms of ***constancy and consistency.*** It is an absolute devotion to keeping one's word. It's ***the glue that holds all relationships together,*** because all relationships require trust, and trust is based on integrity.

Think of Hansie Cronje and his involvement in the 'match-fixing' scandal. When his career came to an end, he didn't lose any of his talent or ability, he lost his integrity. ***People will forgive occasional slips in your ability but one slip in your character could cost you your success.***

V^3 *(VISION - VALUE - VOICE)*

1. Have and update your *VISION*: In this 2005 commencement speech, Apple CEO Steve Jobs told Stanford graduates, "Your time is limited, so don't waste it living someone else's life. Don't be trapped by dogma, which is living with the results of other people's

> "A leader is one who knows the way, goes the way and shows the way."
> John C. Maxwell

thinking. *Do what you love and live your own life."*

What does success look like, sound like and feel like to you? For some, it's climbing the corporate ladder, driving the dream car and having the dream job. For some, it's being a mother or father, husband or wife. For some, it's climbing Everest or travelling the world. For some, like my Mum, it's feeding the homeless and striving to build shelters for the needy. For some success can be measured, for others it's felt. For me, it's a bit of all the above. I want the nice car and comfortable house but I won't feel successful if I haven't achieved it by making a difference in the lives of others. Being a mother and wife is important to me but never at the expense of settling for any relationship. I know what success is for me.

Do you know what success is for you? There is no 'right' or 'wrong' answer. There is only an authentic answer you can live with so that, as Stephen Covey puts it, you *don't end up climbing the ladder of success only to find it's against the wrong wall*. What do you love? What are

> My vision is ...

your top five values? Are you living them? Are you climbing the 'right' ladder of success for you? When did you last update your vision? If I were to ask you to write it down in 20 words or less, would you hesitate or do you know it by heart because you live and breathe it every day?

Are your day-to-day activities in line with achieving your vision? Is your personal vision aligned with your organisational vision? Spend five minutes at the end of every day thinking and planning your activity for the next day. Don't get too bogged down in your day-to-day tasks that you forget to stay on track and set goals in line with your vision. At the end of each day, ask yourself, *"What must I do tomorrow that will make a difference to my boss, the team, my career and my life?"* *Keep your eye on the bigger picture* and your longer-term career goals to avoid getting bogged down in the daily grind and the pressures and stresses of your daily work load.

2. Know your *VALUE*: Once you have determined your values and your vision, (i.e. you know what you want and you know you are going to get there) the tricky part of knowing your value comes into play. *Do you know what you are worth?* Yes, I know you are priceless, that's not what I mean. *I mean, when it comes down to rands and cents, do you know what you are worth? You might be worth more than you think!*

Before I started Key Steps Corporate Training, I had always allowed someone else to determine my worth. Of course, I made sure I earned a decent salary and got market related annual increases but I hadn't really worked out what I was actually worth. *Assigning a real value to my time (one I knew I could deliver every cent of value for) was a very challenging and liberating experience for me.* Do I still sometimes err on giving too much value for too little actual rands and cents? Sometimes. And I'm blessed to do work I love so the reward is actually never less that the effort I put in because I get to experience magic in the shifts others make. But mostly, I know my value and I aim to deliver that plus 10%.

Ever heard the story of the giant ship engine that failed? The ship's owners tried one expert after another, but none of them could figure out how to fix the engine. Then they brought in an old man who had been fixing ships since he was a youngster. He carried a large bag of tools with him, and when he arrived, he immediately went to work. He inspected the engine very carefully, top to bottom. Two of the ship's owners were there, watching this man, hoping he would know what to do. After looking things over, the old man reached into his bag and pulled out a small hammer. He gently tapped on a large pipe. Instantly, the engine lurched into life. He carefully put his hammer away. The engine was fixed!

A week later, the owners received a bill for R 10,000.00.

"What?!" the owners exclaimed. "He hardly did anything!" So they wrote the old man a note saying, "Please send us an itemised bill."

The man sent a bill that read:
Tapping with a hammer R20.00
Knowing where to tap R9,980.00

Successful people know their value and are not afraid to charge what they are worth because they know they do make a difference.

3. Distinguish your *VOICE*: To be successful today, our most important job is to be head marketer for the brand called "YOU". It's that simple... that hard... and that inescapable.

I'd recommend being great for some people rather than trying to please everyone. Do not be afraid to make people react strongly for or against you. It's often said that you're not doing something right unless you're getting under someone's skin. That doesn't mean I recommend you go out there and be a jerk. It just means that *you won't please all the people, all the time, and if you do, you'll end up a mile wide and an inch deep and mediocre to everyone*.

What is your personal brand? When people talk about you what do they say? What are you known for? What makes you different and sets you apart?

| "Glass, china and reputation are easily cracked, and never mended well." Benjamin Franklin |

E^3 *(ENERGY - ENTHUSIASM - EQ)*

1. Use your *ENERGY* wisely: To be truly successful you need to *have a passion to succeed that is tempered by wisdom, experience and ethics*. How many failures have you seen that were the result of apathy or incompetence? Even more

> "Most people never run far enough on their first wind to find out if they've got a second. Give your dreams all you've got and you'll be amazed at the energy that comes out of you."
> William James

poignant are the failures due to untempered energy and passion that leads to bad judgements.

I have very *high energy levels* and these can sometimes wear out the people around me (and even my physical self too!) so I have had to learn to temper them. Maybe you know someone who's the exact opposite and you feel like winding up because they have such *low energy levels* and come across as uncommitted. Basically we need a balance between the two. And *if we have to tip the scales in favour of one... choose high energy levels*. Successful people throughout time usually have extremely high passion and energy levels they have learnt to temper.

2. Never lose your *ENTHUSIASM*: Why is enthusiasm so important to success? The reason is that the difference between success and failure is often minute. *Two people with virtually the same amount of skill and talent can differ vastly in the amount of success they achieve.* This difference can't be attributed to having more ability than the other person. In fact, in many cases, the more successful person actually has less ability. *The main difference is in enthusiasm.* And the ability to get up one more time than they fall down.

3. Improve your *EMOTIONAL QUOTIENT (EQ)*: Emotional Intelligence is the ability to recognise and manage your own emotions and the emotions

> "As much as 80% of adult 'success' comes from EQ."
> Daniel Goleman

of others. *EQ is increasingly recognised as being as important as – if not more important than – Intelligence Quotient (IQ) for success in business, relationships and life in general.* Traditionally, your IQ (the logical, mathematical and linguistic abilities measured by standard IQ tests) was thought to be the full story on how intelligent you are. This older model would suggest that a high IQ is all you need for success. Experience tells us that this is not the whole picture and numerous studies illustrate that something more is definitely needed.

Developing EQ is my passion. It's one of our key workshops, as I know the success other's can achieve by increasing their EQ is unparalleled. *And it not only makes us happier, it makes us able to motivate ourselves, manage stress in our lives and resolve conflict with others.* It gives us the skills to be able to empathise, encourage, comfort, discipline and confront different kinds of people appropriately in different situations. It determines how effectively we express our emotions within the cultural contexts of our family, our workplace and our community. It determines how well people listen to us and how well we are heard. You can't afford not to constantly develop yours! *The amount of success you can have – and mange to keep – is proportional to your EQ.*

So now that we have journeyed and explored how to **THRIVE**[3] together, take a few minutes and recap so you can make sure you are ready to take Key Steps with me today and create your success of tomorrow and the next day and the next day...

What are the three Key Steps that will make the biggest difference to your life and success six months from now?

T	1. Thinking 2. Time 3. Tenacity
H	1. Hope 2. Honesty 3. Help
R	1. Rapport and relationships 2. Rules 3. Results
I	1. Involve 2. Ingenuity 3. Integrity
V	1. Vision 2. Value 3. Voice
E	1. Energy 2. Enthusiasm 3. Emotional Quotient (EQ)

One way or another, every day, ***you CAN and DO make a difference***. Do you want it to be a successful difference for yourself and those you care about? Of course you do, so what are you doing about it?

                'be the difference that makes the ***difference*'

BALANCE YOUR LIFE

WILHELM LOMBARD

Qualifications
M.Phill (PPL), B.Ed, HED, Nas N Dipl, Nas Tech Dipl.
Business Continuity Certificate, Solution Focused Practices Certificate

Wilhelm Lombard is a dynamic communicator with the passion for helping people reaching their full potential in life. With over 25 years experience in various industries and training environments he acts and is qualified as a personal and professional leadership practitioner/facilitator. For several years he was a senior lecturer in the technical college environment, lecturing technical and computer related subjects and courses. He was also involved in the sales and marketing business as well as in the recruitment and placement of people especially in the information technology industry. He is also a qualified Avionic Instrument Technician. He is a registered world teacher at WTB and has completed a three year training curriculum in the "Million Leaders Mandate" initiative under Dr John C Maxwell (Equip).

Wilhelm focuses on total wellness of a company. He firmly believe that companies are not achieving according to their potential because of the mere fact that employees are finding themselves in some or other stage of burnout. Wilhelm's 2-days total wellness (Energy revitalising) workshop has a direct impact on effectiveness, productivity and finally the bottom-line of a business.

> Cell: 082 774 7471
> info@wilhelmlombard.com
> www.wilhelmlombard.com

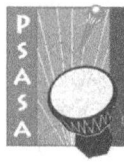

BALANCE YOUR LIFE

What is it that prevents a person from being successful? There may be numerous answers to this question, but in my mind one of the big problems of our time is the lack of energy. If a person  lacks the energy (vitality) to do the things that are necessary to become successful, he/she will simply not achieve success. Since energy is directly related to health, it can be concluded that the healthier you are in all aspects of life, the more energy/power you will have to achieve success.

A quick and preliminary survey of people in my living and working environment revealed that the vast majority of them indeed experience fatigue as a problem. A number of studies focusing on the problem of shortage of energy or chronic fatigue bring the following to light: By and large, when patients are asked if they experience severe problems with fatigue, more than a quarter (25%) say that they consider it a serious problem. Half of these people, approximately 13%, visit their doctor because they lack energy. Of these, about one half (±7%), confirm that chronic fatigue or burnout is the reason for their ailment.

When patients are generally asked about the presence of chronic fatigue, more than 27% confirm that they are experiencing it. Thus, the first question is – what is the reason for this? Answer: A lack of balance in our lives. The second question: What can one do to prevent the loss of energy? Answer: Live a balanced life. Focus on all six basic life dimensions, namely the spiritual, physical, intellectual, emotional, social and professional (work and finance) dimensions. The purpose of this chapter is to help you to become aware of the importance of these life dimensions and to give you some practical guidelines to keep your life in balance.

Spiritual dimension

When a person wants to live a successful life, it is very important to consider a healthy spiritual life. Teilhard de Chardine argues that "We are not human beings with a spiritual experience; we are spiritual beings with a human experience". In this dimension, each person is seeking the meaning of their existence.

Spiritual intelligence can be seen as the way we address issues related to values and meaning in life. It enables us to understand our lives better, particularly our everyday operations in a wider, richer and more meaningful sense. Spiritual intelligence enables us to make a distinction between actions and choices because we know what the best outcomes will be. Zohar and Marshall (*Spiritual Intelligence: The Ultimate Intelligence*) affirm that spiritual intelligence is the foundation for the effective functioning of cognitive intelligence (IQ) and emotional intelligence (EQ). They indicate that spiritual intelligence (SQ) is the intelligence of your soul and your being, and that we use our spiritual intelligence to heal ourselves.

Spiritual intelligence implies that humans have a choice to decide whether they want to be in a certain situation or not.

 Hence one has the ability to create a situation or even to change to a better situation. Spiritual intelligence is the process of dialogue between rational thinking and emotions and it also facilitates communication between the spirit and the body. It creates the basis for growth and transformation to operate from a meaningful centre.

By monitoring the boundaries of the situation, one can establish and manage it. Spiritual intelligence relates to the following abilities:

- To experience religion, partly to get yourself committed to something larger than yourself.
- To experience meaningfulness and find value in people and things.
- To live a purposeful life.
- To experience inner growth.
- To be able to handle crises and border situations.
- To understand our true self and what things mean to us.
- To realise and to reach out to our true potential.
- To be aware of existential problems and to handle them.

To be spiritually intelligent in a world that is spiritually dumb requires the following from you:

- Be aware of your own deep life goals.
- Be aware of your deepest motives.
- Develop a lifestyle that takes your own needs and those of the people around you (your family) into account.
- Experience peace.
- Make time for things that are important.
- Develop a high degree of self-awareness.
- Be aware of and respond to your deepest self.
- Develop the ability to overcome difficulties and use them to your benefit.
- Work at the ability to stand alone against others for something in which you believe (values).
- Refuse to cause harm and hurt in the world (Zohar & Marshall, 2000:284).

You demonstrate spiritual intelligence or spiritual leadership when you:

- Experience purpose in your life.
- Experience personal wellness.
- Live in peace and harmony with yourself.
- Are in contact with your deeper self.
- Live with hope and positive expectations.
- Live a service-orientated and unselfish lifestyle.
- Live for a greater purpose than just the self.
- Can appreciate simplicity, beauty and goodness.
- Have enthusiasm for life.

Spiritual well-being

This aspect involves more than the mere following of a religion or specific religious belief. It consists of concepts from different disciplines (psychology, sociology, philosophy and theology) that all together lead to certain personality traits and results. These qualities empower the individual to handle the challenges of life better and to experience greater purpose in life – which eventually leads to success.

Spiritual well-being involves:

- A set of ethical rules by which a person lives.
- A feeling of unselfishness and a sensitivity for other people.
- A commitment to a "supreme being".

Spiritual well-being is also something that acts on the other dimensions to ensure health. Finally it serves as a catalyst of energy, which is crucial for success.

The consequences of a reduced level of spiritual well-being seem to create a state of 'unbalance' between other dimensions, which leads to a lack of energy/health. The spiritual aspect of health is much more than just one of the six dimensions mentioned earlier. It may also provide the supporting mechanism with which the other five dimensions articulate and interact with each other. Willa Bowels (1993:84) makes a very insightful remark in her article "How to get quick energy" when she says: "Breaking God's laws and avoiding repentance to receive forgiveness brings a sense of condemnation that will affect every area of your Life. Forgiving yourself, all others, and accepting God's love, mercy and forgiveness is the first step to a happy and energetic life."

Physical dimension

The physical dimension is the visual dimension and the dimension that is noticed first. It entails the physical activity and

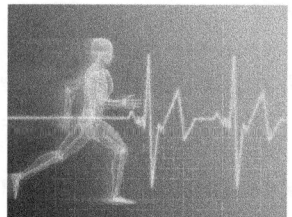

ability of man. The body gives man the opportunity to participate in a unique and recognisable manner to perform his task on earth. The body consists of 75 trillion cells and not many people are aware that health starts and ends within each of these body cells. To sustain a healthy and energetic body, three vital processes that involve the cell have to be kept going, namely:

- **Innervation** – the provision of energy (nerve supply) from the brain via the spinal cord to each cell.
- **Nutrition** – the supply of nutrients to the cell.
- **Drainage** – the disposal of waste from the cell.

Innervation
Anything that prevents the nerve impulses going to and from the cell or that obstructs the supply of energy, has an impact on the health of the cell. Vitality is reduced due to overwork, night work, bad habits like smoking and alcohol consumption, overstimulation, side effects of medication, fatigue, poor medical treatment, mechanical factors, negative thinking, fear,

tension, stress and bad moods. All of these weaken nutrition to the cell, thus leading to low vitality and consequently to disease/loss of energy.

Nutrition
Each cell must have the necessary blood, white blood cells (lymph) and other essential nutrients provided to it to function effectively. Most dieticians agree that a balanced diet that includes a bit of all the food groups (meat and other proteins, vegetables, fruits and different grains and fibres) provides the best nutrition. Abnormal distribution and composition of life-saving nutrients manifest as the primary cause of illness and loss of vitality. Wrong eating habits cause imbalances in the blood and lymph composition, as well as a lack of the necessary elements (such as mineral salts in organic form), which then lead to malfunctioning of the cell.

Drainage
Inadequate drainage of waste, leading to blockages that impede blood and lymphatic flow, is the third primary cause of illness and fatigue. The accumulation of wastes and toxins is caused by low vitality (activity); a fatty diet; overeating; the use of alcoholic and narcotic stimulants, drugs and vaccines; the suppression of acute illnesses with medication that has side effects; and surgical operations – all of which cause the cell to malfunction.

A low level of vitality causes a slow vibration or frequency of the atoms in the cell, which results in a decreased resistance and inadequate drainage or disposal of hazardous materials, poisons, germs and parasites. A positive condition (physical exercise) implies high vitality and an intense atom vibration, which leads to high immunity (resistance to diseases). What happens is this: The higher the supply of life force, the higher the intensity of the vibration activity of the atoms and molecules in the cells of organs and tissue, thus increasing the output of toxins (which cause the destruction of cells). Hence, the greater the flow of vitality (life force) into the organism, the better its vitality and the larger its physical strength and positive resistance – this eventually results in more energy being made available to ensure a successful life.

Health or disease is fundamentally present in each cell. The cell is a living unit that can on its own eat, drink, grow, get rid of waste, multiply, get outdated, and die – like man in his totality. If the individual cell is healthy and possesses a high degree of vitality, then the total person is healthy and capable of living a healthy and successful life. Therefore, physical exercise, eating the right food, drinking enough water and not allowing all kinds of bad things to enter the body, are essentials for success. On the other hand, if the vibration activity of the cell decreases due to a reduction in vitality associated with the natural aging process (people becoming less active by choice) or in an artificial way by wrong thought processes (negative thoughts), bad lifestyle, overwork, unnatural stimulation and various other adverse impacts, the body will not be healthy and this will have an enormous effect on your success.

Intellectual dimension

The intellectual dimension refers primarily to the cognitive ability of each person, namely to function rationally. Cognitive ability  involves logical and linear thinking. "It is goal orientated, how-to thinking, and the kind with which we manage the rules of grammar or a game." (Zohar) The brain has a huge impact on human health. Pearsall warns us about the selfishness of the brain, but also admits that the strength of our thinking is a very important partner, especially when we keep psychoneuroimmunology in mind. "We know now that no body system, including the complex immune system, works entirely on its own and independently of the other body systems. All body system functions are coordinated by the brain. Neuro-linguistic programming can play a very big role in the rephrasing of negative experiences or situations." Ralph Waldo Emerson aptly remarked that "the ancestor to every action is a thought."

The body, mind and brain relation

The study of how the brain influences the immune system or immune cells through behaviour, is called psychoneuroimmunology (PNI). It was found that there is a definite connection between the mind, what one thinks and the immune system. Many years ago already doctors determined that disease follows after episodes of frustration. Egyptian physicists prescribed a positive attitude as a way to prevent disease. A half millennium before the birth of Christ, Hippocrates (the father of medicine) warned physicians that to be able to heal patients, they required knowledge of "the whole of things", that is knowledge of the mind **and** the body. PNI focuses on the relationship between the mind and the immune system. It is argued that a positive attitude, such as a sense of control, acts in some cases as an antidote to disease. The American psychologist Walter Cannon carried out a series of experiments early in the 20th century that provided physical evidence that certain glands in the body respond to stress. His experiments demonstrated the relationship between stress and the hypothalamus, the pituitary gland (in the middle of the head – just below the brain) and adrenalin glands.

Hormones secreted by the endocrine glands control all tissue and every organ in the body. This mixture of hormones is controlled by the pituitary gland. The output of the pituitary hormones is controlled by both chemical releases and nerve impulses from the neighbouring part of the brain called the hypothalamus. The pituitary gland regulates many of the body's unconscious processes such as heartbeat, respiration, blood pressure, temperature, etc.

When the worries of modern life result in a constant state of stress, the body's resistance against disease weakens. This leads to a reduction in vitality, which results in a loss of energy. The hormones in the body that are released as a result of stress, suppress the immune system in such a way that a person lacks energy.

Our thoughts consequently have a direct impact on our vitality. Our emotions and our words let the body know what we expect of it. By visualising certain changes, we can help the body to reflect them. Our thoughts and emotions have a huge impact on the inflow and distribution of the necessary life force. Things like fear, sadness and other negative emotions cause a freezing effect. These destructive vibrations paralyse the body's essential activities. All destructive emotional vibrations (caused by impatience, irritability, anger and hatred, etc.) prevent the inflow of life force through the body. However, constructive emotions like faith, hope, happiness, love, and a sense of caring for others have a relaxing, harmonising and energising effect on the tissues of the body.

Emotional dimension

The emotional dimension is the dimension where wonderful opportunities open up the moment that we recognise and  manage them. Emotions generate this energy that gets us 'moving' (into motion). We can't help responding to our emotions. They just happen to us, rather than the things that we 'will' to occur. Emotions happen mainly at the level of the subconscious. For instance, happiness, joy and laughter, cause the release of endorphins. Endorphins are powerful opiates that make you feel good. They boost your immune system, relax muscles, elevate your mood and dampen pain. Adrenalin releases when you feel fear, anxiety or stress. It causes blood vessels to dilate, making your skin flush. Rapid, shallow breathing ensues. Muscles tighten, especially around the stomach and shoulder area.

The purpose of adrenalin is to place your body in a high-alert rapid-response fight-or-flight state. In emergencies, this is beneficial, as it aids escape. But, over a long period, adrenalin can be very damaging to your body. It suppresses your immune system, impairs digestion, uses up vital vitamins and minerals, causes pain and stiffness, makes your body acidic resulting in inflammation, and drains vitality.

It ties in with the observation made by Hafen, namely that "90% of all health problems can be traced, at least in part, to the influence of emotions". What is important is that it is not the emotion itself that we experience, but how we react to it. Salovey provides a few guidelines on how to manage our emotions:

- Know your own emotions – be self-aware, in other words, know the feeling when it happens.
- Manage your emotions – only when a person is aware of his/her emotions, he/she can manage and control them.
- Motivate yourself – use positive emotions to motivate you, to think more creatively and to reduce impulsive behaviour. Become more productive and effective in everything you do.
- Recognise emotions in others – help them to gain self-knowledge (self-awareness) of their own emotions and show empathy for others' feelings.
- Handle relationships – manage emotions in other people's lives.
- Handle people with care.

The above indicates the path of emotional intelligence. The emotional dimension is the dimension where especially the role of the heart is discussed, the so-called "L" force. Arthur A. Stone, psychologist at the State University of New York Medical School found that whereas negative emotions can reduce a person's immunity, small joys or pleasures can improve immunity. He researched 100 men for three months and found that stress weakens the immune system for one day, but fun and positive events enhance the immune system for two days. The decrease in the normal number of positive events made volunteers more susceptible to colds due to an increase in normal stressful experiences. Dr Aristo Wojdani, director of the Immunoscience Laboratory in Los Angeles, confirmed the above in that he found in his studies that both positive and negative events affect the immune system.

He found that stress, fear, grief and sad experiences suppressed the immune system for twenty hours after the experience of oppression, while positive experiences strengthened the immune system for up to three days after the positive experience. As mentioned, the brain contains tremendous healing power and by linking the power of the brain and the heart to the body, miraculous healing powers can be unlocked so that the cause of illness and fatigue can be prevented. The key lies not in what emotions we experience, but in how we react to it. There is a positive way in which to deal with all negative emotions. All emotions – even negative ones – have a purpose and can lead to a positive outcome; it just depends on how they are handled.

Several studies have demonstrated that positive emotions increase immunity and thus protect health, but that negative emotions decrease immunity and lead to disease. This phenomenon is partly responsible for the increase in illness and loss of life among people who have recently lost a partner. Researchers at Mount Sinai Medical School had blood tests done on men whose wives died. They found that their immune functioning was suppressed and that there was a clear decrease in white blood cells that protect the body against disease. It took a full year for their immune systems to return to their normal functioning. In today's life people need to cope with so many intrigues like divorce, crime, corruption and other traumas that their immune systems are under constant attack. The immune system consists of more than a dozen different white blood cells that are concentrated in the spleen, thymus gland and lymph glands. These white blood cells patrol the entire body through the blood and lymph systems. They are divided into two main types, called B-cells and T-cells. B-cells produce chemical substances that neutralise toxins which cause toxic disease organisms, while they help the body to produce its own defence system. The T-cells comprise "killer" cells and their helpers who destroy bacteria and viruses. It seems essential that one should realise the extreme importance of becoming aware of one's emotions and the responsibility that one has to manage emotions in the right way so as to be successful in life.

Social dimension

One of man's main features is the fact that he is a relationship creature. The need for interaction with other people is one of the ground motives of human existence. The enormous  influence on us of the people around us cannot be over emphasised. However, even among crowds of people one can be very alone. It is said that loneliness is the greatest unrecognised contributor to premature death in the United States. Social wellness means having positive interaction and enjoying being with others. It involves being comfortable and at ease during work and leisure situations, and being able to communicate one's feelings and needs to others. It also involves developing and building close and intimate friendships, practising empathy and effective listening, caring for others and for the common good, and allowing others to care for you. Social wellness means recognising the need for leisure and recreation and budgeting time for those activities.

Social wellness facts:

- Socially isolated people are more susceptible to illness and the death rate among them is two to three times higher than among those who are not socially isolated.
- People who maintain their social network and support systems do better under stress.
- Touching, stroking and hugging can improve health.
- Laughter really is good medicine.
- Cholesterol levels go up when human companionship is lacking.
- Warm, close friendships cause higher levels of immunoglobulin A (an antibody) that helps keep away respiratory infections.
- A strong social network can create a good mood and enhance self-esteem.

So how can I improve my social wellness?

- Practise self-disclosure.
- Get to know your personal needs and pursue things and people who nurture those needs.
- Contact and make a specific effort to talk to the people who are supportive in your life.
- Attend a wellness forum.
- Join a club or organisation that interests you.

To climb the mountain of success is impossible on your own. Really successful people have a support system. Loneliness drains the vital energy that you need to be successful.

Professional dimension

The last of the six basic life dimensions is the professional or work dimension. It is within this dimension that everyone of us gets the opportunity to add value to life. It is ironic and unfortunate that so many people who spend so much time on their profession or work are unhappy and do not experience fulfillment. For most people, their primary task on earth is to give content to the professional dimension. When Stephen Covey advises us that we need to live, love, learn and leave a legacy, we realise that we can accomplish all four of these aspects in this dimension, especially the latter. The impact of the professional dimension in people's lives is often underestimated. Christine Wicker asks in her article *Seeking the Soul of Business* if people are truly happy at work, because "that's  where people spend most of their time" (Wicker, 2001:247). It is essential that people experience meaning and purpose in what they do.

Conclusion
It is not difficult to realise the important role that each of the different dimensions plays in terms of one's health in general and vitality in particular. A prerequisite for individual success is therefore that a person should experience optimal functioning in all six dimensions. Underlying factors that contribute to success must be present, such as challenges to the mental, management of emotions, food for the physical, love of the social and a sense of meaning and purpose in the professional dimension.

In conclusion, to lead a healthy and energetic life, it is necessary for us to realise that life is an ongoing, dynamic process where everyone is responsible for developing his/her own potential and for maximising the self in all six dimensions. This determines not only our quality of life, but also whether we will achieve success in the long run.

PASSION IS SUCCESS

WOLFGANG RIEBE

Wolfgang Riebe, change management guru, best selling author, international keynote speaker and comedy illusionist, is a world leader when it comes to changing attitudes, inspiration and motivation.

He has inspired millions of people worldwide with appearances in over **125 countries** – from Hollywood to Singapore. He was the star of numerous television shows and many of his own prime time TV series, coupled with **25 years experience** in the speaking, service and entertainment industry, plus his **Ph.D in Communications**, make him a world leader in his field.

Wolfgang is fluent in English, German and Afrikaans and often also fulfills the role of '3-in-1' man, hosting entire conferences as the speaker, emcee and entertainer. He is the **2010/2011 National President** of the **Professional Speakers Association of Southern Africa**.

"Greatness in a Speaker, is defined by passion, humility, sincerity and personal experience, coupled with his ability to capture, communicate and entertain his audience, while still sharing practical, sustainable and immediately implementable life skills which have a positive effect on all present."　　　　　　　　**Dr Wolfgang Riebe**

Cell: 082 357 4446
info@wolfgangriebe.com
www.wolfgangriebe.com

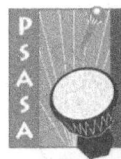

PASSION IS SUCCESS

My first question to you is, "How do you wake up in the morning?" Is it a case of opening your eyes, not feeling your best, groaning and saying to yourself, "Oh no, another damn day!" Or, do you jump out of bed, give your partner next to you, and the cat, a huge fright as you shout, "Yes! Wow, another amazing day. So much to do and so little time!"

I take it that for most people, the first example is the norm. People just aren't excited about life anymore. Just sit on the London underground and look at everyone's faces. Too few smile. If you do smile at someone, odds are you will get arrested for being a public nuisance. It's the same in the traffic in any city in the morning – just look at the faces of the people in the cars next to you – how many are smiling? It's as if the majority of people today have lost the will to live and have fun in life.

Once many years back, I actually met someone who had passion. I was sitting in the peak hour morning traffic on the M25 around London, when the man in the car next to me suddenly held up a board which read, "Hi, great morning, isn't it?" In fact he had a whole conversation with everyone around him using these boards. He had found a way to make the traffic fun!

As an inspirational speaker I find it very worrying that there are so many passionless people out there. I have conducted much research as to why people don't live life to the full, and trust that my insights will help you discover your passion once more.

I am constantly reminded of a saying by an unknown author:

> **Life is like a roll of toilet paper.**
> **The closer it gets to the end, the faster it goes.**

Isn't that so true? The older we get, the faster time seems to go? Even the children of today are commenting that their days fly by. Surely then, if this is the case, why doesn't humanity make the most of every moment they have, seeing that all goes by so fast?

My aim today, is threefold. Firstly, I want to identify what passion is, then explain why the majority of people have lost it, and finally share with you how you can discover your passion again.

WHAT IS PASSION?

I have found the following definition on the net, and curiously enough some examples say it is Cher's definition, while others claim it belongs to Madonna. Either way, this is what one of these ladies have to say, when asked how they would define passion:

"There are a number of mechanical devices which increase sexual arousal, particularly in women. Chief among these is the Mercedes-Benz 380SL convertible."

However, that's not quite the passion I am talking about! It is that drive and lust for life that is important to me. It's what makes you smile when things aren't going your way.

Next step was to look at the Oxford English Dictionary definition:

Passion: "a strong feeling, or enthusiasm."

I have always said that I love life, and feel that love and passion are closely linked. Hence I checked out the definition of love as well.

Love: "have a strong affection, or deep tender feelings for."

Isn't that interesting? Both definitions are pretty similar. The bottom line here is that love and passion are closely linked. They feed off each other. Think about it for a moment. If I am in love with someone, passion always forms part of that relationship. If I am passionate about a sport or hobby in life, I really love doing it. In the same vein, have you ever met someone really successful, who seems to be having fun at their job? Ask them why they do it. Odds are that they will reply, "It's my passion, I absolutely love it!"

You will notice that these people also never see their careers as work, but as an extension of themselves. They don't work nine to five, but rather 24/7, 365. They don't need a vacation, as what they do, is so inspiring for them, they never get tired.

As a keynote speaker and entertainer, people often ask me whether I get nervous on stage, or tired of travelling around the world. Huh? Why? I love what I do! If you didn't quite get what I mean, I'll repeat it for you, "I love what I do!" Even though there have been tough times, and times when the work wasn't plentiful, I always have fun. I have often said, "I cannot believe that people pay me to have fun!" I firmly believe that this is a philosophy which everyone can have... if they truly love what they do.

This we will identify as the final chapter in this book. But first and foremost, as with any problems in life, one must identify the root, or cause of the problem, and ask ourselves, "Why have we lost our passion?"

WHY WE LOST IT?

This is not an academic thesis, hence I will not become long winded and share ten different schools of thought based on various hypotheses! I could... but I won't.
In a nutshell, most people have lost their passion due to expectations!

That's it, there is no more to it. It's as simple as that!

Expectations are the root of all problems!

We live in a society of instant gratification and expectations. What do I mean? Think about it... few people do anything today without expecting something in return. I work because I expect a salary. I ask someone out on a date because I expect (hope) to have sex. I make an appointment with a potential client, because I want (expect) them to buy my product. I will pick up your children from school because I expect you to do the same for me next week. I'll do the dishes for you tonight honey because I expect some action in the bedroom later. When I am born and I scream as a baby, immediately I must get milk or have my nappy changed... instant gratification.

Get the point? Too few just do things out of the kindness of the their heart. It's all about, "What's in it for me?"

Don't get me wrong, there are many people who don't follow the above example – but, those are the passionate ones! Those are the people that are enjoying their life and living every moment to the full.

I am merely trying to answer the question for you personally, why the passion has gone. Think about it, we have been brought up and conditioned in a society where 'expectation' is the norm. As a child you were conditioned to behave. If you behaved, you got things. In school we were taught to learn and pass our grades. In return we received our diploma. Then we had to study at university to get a degree, so that we could get a good job, etc. Expectations, expectations, expectations!

We have been intrinsically conditioned to expect. But, and it's a big BUT, in reality things do not always work out the way we expect! That's when disappointment takes over and we start losing the zest and passion for life. If you really think about it logically, it's a system that is bound to fail.

Add to this, the greed of big business corporations and the manipulation of the media. What chance do you have to be positive? Take the media reporting on an accident. The front page headline reads:

2 KILLED IN HORROR CRASH

A typical headline. Sensationalist, negative and attention grabbing. That same headline could read:

AMBULANCE HEROES ARRIVE IN UNDER 2 MINUTES

This is more positive and instils hope. But, according to the majority of journalists, it won't sell. It's not sensationalist enough. I have constantly challenged the press and media on the above, and maintain that if they only put the positive spin on any story (every story has two sides), within three weeks the entire city, or country will have a more positive attitude.

If you think I am being unrealistic, just read the first three pages of any newspaper. It's all about politics, politicians and their antics. 90% of what is written will never come to pass, but it sells! Take a society magazine reporting on celebrity lifestyles... I cannot believe that people actually read such rubbish. Then they wonder why they are negative. Hello... smell the roses.

People actually try to emulate well-known personalities who are so screwed-up in their heads, simply because the media gives them attention. I will never understand this. Take a popular American pop star who shaved all the hair off her head. This woman, in my opinion, is a nutcase. Do you have any idea how many people copied her? And it didn't stop there, she still has a huge following today. Huh? And all these people wonder why their lives are not working out.

How many women try to have Barbie doll figures? Why do you think you still see weight loss adverts constantly on television? In fact, a researcher did a study, and concluded that if any woman did have a Barbie doll figure, her back would break. It wouldn't be able to support her chest!

Recently, a stepson of a celebrity committed a crime. What did the press do? There were headlines nationwide with the celebrity's name in big print, about the crimes of a stepson which he hadn't seen or heard of in years. Whose name sold the paper? Whose name was damaged in the process?

Enough, I am sure you get the gist of what I am saying. Vulgar and perverse are the operative words here. It is perverse that the media and society has dictated how we need to feel and think. Occasionally there is an exposé about something bad that has happened. In many cases it is an eye blind and just leads to more problems. A great example is the 2009 recession. Governments worldwide cried wolf and claimed that excessive debts and too much credit was partly to blame. And everyone accepted that they were also to blame because of excessive debts.

Once again, the blame had been shifted to the people. Let me ask you a question and I want you to think about it carefully. Try to come up with your own answer. Name the one organisation/company in the world, or your own country, that is totally useless? In other words, it doesn't generate any income whatsoever. It merely spends, and most of the time cannot do that efficiently either.

Got the answer yet? The government!

Interestingly enough, years ago no-one got the answer immediately. Today if I pose the question to a live audience, the answer is shouted out unanimously and instantly!

Back to the debt problem. Where does a government get its money from? The taxes which you and I pay. They will only get taxes from you if you work and earn money. You will only work to earn money if you have debt (mortgage, car, etc.) If you have no debt, you don't have to work. Please understand that I am not being anti-government here, but am merely trying to put the economics of everything into perspective.

Back to the above recession scenario. The governments blame excessive debt as the problem. Who is it that wants us to have debt so that we must work and pay taxes? The government! Yet via the media, they want to shift the blame to the masses. Get my point? Many governments have now implemented 'Credit Acts' to legitimise these claims and 'protect' the consumer. Interesting... the banks are still giving out loans, cars are still being sold and all these people are still making profits.

Now you want to know why you wake up depressed and are no longer passionate about life? I trust I have highlighted an angle, and made you realise that humanity is completely controlled and manipulated by 'the powers that be.' Unfortunately, not everyone has the will, or insight to realise this, and hence they fall into the rat race. The rat race is dominated by fear, and it is this fear that also breaks us down.

> ## Remember, that even if you win the rat race, you are still a rat!

Look at children today. When I was a child I always 'wanted'. I wanted a sweet, I wanted a new train set. Listen to the kids today and how they speak to their parents. They no longer 'want' they 'need'! If you have your own children, listen to them and you will see that it is all about 'needing'. I 'need' money for the tuck-shop at school today. Listen to them, and you will see that I speak the truth. This is how the media have brainwashed the youngsters of today.

I need! If I don't get it, my need has been denied. That's far worse than a 'want' being denied! Get my point?

We have been conditioned not to understand the difference between 'pleasure' and 'joy' anymore. In fact, the media has made everyone believe that these two terms are identical, when if fact thoy differ hugely.

It is once you understand the difference between these two concepts, that you can begin re-discovering your passion.

Pleasure is derived from things outside ourselves – materialism. It is temporary. What is pleasure today can be sorrow tomorrow.

Joy arises from within ourselves and is a state of consciousness. It is giving attention. Ask yourself – whatever you are doing, is there lightness, laughter, ease in what you are doing right now. If there isn't, then you are living in future or past time, but not in the present moment. To find JOY, realise, it is 'HOW' you do things.

A person who is passionate and has a love for life, experiences joy in everything that they do.

It is important that you understand that 'temporary' things cannot bring you joy, but only pleasure for a limited time only. Here are some temporary things in life: Car, home, computer, PSP, eating out, spouse and children.

What! How can my spouse and children be temporary? Of course they are. One day your spouse will die and you will be left alone. The same applies to your children. They will grow up and leave the house. The times you spend with them are defined as the 'pleasure principle' and that applies to all the fun things you do. You derive pleasure at that moment.

Joy does come into the picture, only if you create memories with your spouse and children. One day when you retire and think back on your life, what will your memories be? The first car you bought, the newest quad-core computer system you had to take out a loan for? I doubt it. The memories of joy you will have, will be that first kiss, the first steps your child took.

Most people run around so much in the rat race, they only have time for 'quick fixes' and instant gratification. They forget to live and create lasting memories which will bring joy. Can you sit quietly in a room with your spouse and do and say nothing... and enjoy every moment of it? Most people cannot do this! They need to make that moment 'pleasant' by doing something. This is what society and the media has taught them. Why do you think your parents said to you as a child, "I cannot believe how quick you are growing up!"

The person who understands the concept of joy, can however savour the presence of their spouse in that moment. They can be content in the fact that they are simply sharing the same space, and each others company. They can appreciate the deeper spiritual meaning of that moment and keep it as a good memory. Someone once said, "The simple walks with my father around the block on summer nights when I was a child, did wonders for me as an adult." Isn't that what it's really all about?

Here are some thoughts by an unknown author which puts it all into perspective:

- **Today we have higher buildings and wider highways, but shorter temperaments and narrower points of view.**
- **We spend far more, but enjoy far less.**
- **We have bigger houses, but smaller families.**
- **We have more compromises, but less time.**
- **We have more knowledge, but less judgement.**
- **We have modern medicines, but less health.**
- **We have multiplied our possessions, but reduced our values.**
- **We talk way to much, we love only a little, and we hate too much.**
- **We have reached the Moon and come back,**

  but we find it too difficult to cross our own street and meet our neighbours.
- **We claim to have conquered outer space, but not our inner space.**
- **These are times with more freedom and liberty, but less joy....**
- **We have higher incomes, but less morals....**
- **We have much more food and a larger variety of foods , but less nutrition....**
- **Today... two salaries reach home, but divorces increase.**
- **These are times of finer, bigger and more expensive houses, but more broken homes.**

And let's not forget, we have been conditioned to pass the blame onto others, whether it is the previous government, our parents, or our school. Very few people actually take responsibility for their actions. If you don't believe me, just look at any politician being interviewed on television. It's always someone else's fault. They condition everyone else to pass on the blame. Something goes wrong at work, who gets the blame?

It is very rare to see someone own up and accept the blame themselves. When it does happen, it comes as a shock to everyone around them. Huh? And I am not just blaming politicians here. Look around you, your social circle, work colleagues, even your children.

We have been brought up in a society where no-one wants to accept any blame for their mistakes. The greatest example is when people give money to invest in companies. Something goes wrong, like a market crash, and the blame is shifted to others. Here's a tip for you...

The people who really make money are those that inform themselves about investing. Instead of watching sport, or TV every night, they actually educate themselves about the financial markets. Within a short space of time they understand it, and are in control of all their own investments. Remember, as long as you let other people invest your money for you - you will never make any real profits.

There are commissions and costs that must be deducted. You get what's left... if you are lucky. Take the responsibility yourself. It's much more satisfying when you are in control of your own destiny!

Bottom line, unless YOU accept full responsibility for your own life and everything that has and will happen in the future, you will never find joy and passion.

If anything, YOU MUST first accept full responsibility of your own life.

In order to do this and find your passion again, there are a number of things you need to understand.

WHERE DO I FIND MY PASSION AGAIN?

In your own life:

Acceptance

The most important issue, is that you have to accept what has happened in your life up to today. Until you have reached that point, you cannot move further. Accept that what is done is done, and that the past cannot be changed. Also, accept that the world happens to work the way it does, whether you agree with everything or not.

You cannot change the world, BUT – you can change one person through your behaviour towards them, and via the snowball effect, they will in turn affect others positively.

This can be done by following a few simple principles.

Firstly, learn to love! Above all, learn to love yourself and accept who you are as a person. Stop comparing yourself to what society says you have to be. You will never be content or happy within yourself if you try to be like everybody else. Become aware of how society is conditioned. I call people, 'Sheeples'. Why? Because they follow others and copy what everybody else does. Isn't that what sheep do?

Become aware of how the media and society control your thinking. Some things you may agree with, others not. But make sure you know the difference and negate all the negatives in your life.

Earlier I mentioned that it is expectation that breaks down our passion. Hence, when learning to love again, practise 'Unconditional Love'. This stems from within and is all about 100% giving. In other words, whatever you do in life, do it with purity of thought and from the heart. Of course this is not always easy... or is it? You will find that there are some things that are not easy to do like this, and others are. Interestingly enough, you will discover that the easy things, are those that you have an affiliation to. In other words, things you enjoy.

There is no way that anyone can be happy and content if they do things they do not enjoy. I have met so many people stuck in jobs they hate, and the day they retire they start enjoying their hobby. A few years down the line their hobby has become a booming business and they are happier than ever before. Unfortunately many die soon afterwards as well, due to ill health and age. The moral of the story: In their old age they found what they really wanted to do, while they lived an entire life of unhappiness.

If you really enjoy something, do it. Yes, it may well be tough in the beginning, but at least you are enjoying life. Look at it this way. As a child I was an amateur magician, and loved doing tricks. When I finished school I wanted to become a professional entertainer, much to the dismay of my family. I gave in and studied my degree and tried the nine to five career move. I hated every minute and held out for four years. Eventually my conscience made me leave the secure job only to end-up walking the streets of London, looking for gigs as a magician. Two years later I was leading a life of luxury on cruise ships. Eight years later I had seen the entire world and made loads of money.

Why?

Not because I was the best, but because I loved what I was doing. Putting in 18 hours a day, 24/7 was not even a question to me. I enjoyed what I did. The biggest drawcard was that everyone around me saw that I loved what I did, which made me 'appear' to be better than the other magicians. People saw my excitement - it rubbed off onto them. Who do you think people would rather deal with? Someone with a long face, or someone who radiates passion? I trust I have made my point. It's a win win situation, everyone that dealt with me was happy, and so was I.

I do not see myself different to anyone else, except for one thing... my attitude. You just need to change your mind set and have the right attitude and the world is at your feet.

However, the most important point of all... unconditional love. Where does that fit in? When you are doing what you enjoy and love doing, you do it because you want to. You do it because it gives you internal satisfaction. Whether you make money from it or not, is not the driving the force. The driving force is the enjoyment of it. Therefore, you do it without expectation, in other words, unconditionally.

You do it without any expectations. Hence, you cannot be disappointed, as there is no ulterior motive. But, the laws of the universe work in such a way that because you have this attitude, it will send everything back your way. And because you had no expectations, it becomes a surprise and makes you more positive.

There is a great saying:

"A person's true character is revealed by what he does when no one is watching."

Are you a different person when no-one is watching? Then you are not following your passion in life. I trust that makes sense.

In the same vein, another great saying goes:

> **"If you tell a lie, don't believe it deceives**
> **only the other person."**

In other words, if you lie to yourself, it deceives you as well!

So imagine (in the words of John Lennon) for one moment that everyone in the world gave out of pure unconditional love, without expectation... don't you think the world would change overnight? And it can happen. It all starts with you!

Expanding on the above, I am sure you must be familiar with the concept that your body listens to your thoughts. What you think, you are! If you are negative and down, your outer self image shows it. Look at people around you and try identify their moods. It becomes quite easy after a while. When others see you, do they see a positive or negative person? You can try hide it, but it doesn't work. Your internal thoughts always show in your outer body language.

Thus, even if you lie to yourself and attempt to display a positive self image, it doesn't work. The real you lies in your subconscious mind, and try as you want, you cannot deceive it. It is imperative that you are brutally honest with yourself and identify the true inner you. Only then will true happiness follow.

Attachment

There is a great saying, "The best way to keep something is to give it away to others!" However, this does not specifically refer to materialistic items! It is about everything around you. If you give out love, love will come back to you. If you give out hatred, it too will overrun your life.

Attaching yourself to past events, or bad experiences leads to imprisonment and totally limits your possibilities. You are doing yourself great damage by holding onto the past. Remember that nothing in life is permanent. If you hold onto loved ones, money, lifestyle etc. you are attaching and limiting yourself. By living in the moment and savouring every minute of your life you start understanding the concept of happiness:

Living with a belief in a future heaven, only creates a present hell.

Most people live in the past, or the future. Please bear in mind that NOTHING has ever happened in the past or future. Anything that is going to happen to you is going to happen now! Let me explain. The past you cannot change, what happened then is over. There is nothing you can do about it. You can plan for the future, but that's tomorrow. It is not now. And when you reach tomorrow, then that becomes now.

Living fully in the now, makes every memory of yesterday a good one and hence makes the future look more positive.

How do you identify whether your are living in the past or future? Easy. If you are suffering from anxiety, stress, unease and tension, you are living in the future. If you are suffering from guilt, regret, grief, sadness and bitterness, then you are living in the past.

Fair enough, it's easier said than done. But ask yourself, "Will this matter one year from now? How about one month? One week? One day?" If it won't matter in the future, then drop it!

By living your life one day at a time, you live all the days of your life.

Surrender

To many people it means something negative, i.e. giving up. Failing to rise to the challenges of life! That is totally wrong! The true meaning of surrender can be defined in two sentences:

- Yielding to rather than opposing the flow of life, i.e. accepting what is happening without judgement or resistance.
- By surrendering, you end the continual assessing of your mind, i.e. your mind no longer controls you and is no longer your master.

It is therefore who you truly are – it is a state of being! In this state you WILL clearly see what has to be done. It is NOT being cut off from your feelings, but realising with deep inner peace, that what is done, cannot be undone. In other words, we constantly fight against what is going on in the world by becoming aggressive, depressed, moaning etc. This causes us to become negative and subjective, resulting in our actions being emotion driven.

By surrendering yourself to the fact that this is the world you live in, with all its problems, and accepting this, you no longer fight against it and become internally angry. Rather you can now put yourself outside the situation and look at everything objectively, rather than subjectively and realistically decide what role to play in order to begin making a positive difference.

A classic example here was Mother Theresa. She refused to take part in a march against war. The whole concept of war has a negative vibe. Rather, she would take part in a peace march. Why? Peace is more tranquil and sends a message of peace, rather than a message of war. By surrendering, your approach to negative things becomes more positive.

Therefore, when you surrender – you find joy! When Joy comes – unconditional Love comes.

At work

Let us look at a typical example in the work place. The majority of people today work in to pay bills and survive. No matter how I try to put things into perspective and try and make you follow your passion, there will always be those of you that won't change and follow your heart. There is nothing I can do about it. I must surrender myself to this fact. However, that doesn't mean that I should give up and not try, as there will always be those of you that actually follow through with these life lessons I am imparting. That alone is more than enough reason for me to do so.

Therefore, those of you who do not enjoy work and have issues with work colleagues, remember the following points:

"That under everyone's hard shell is someone who wants to be appreciated and loved."

"Opportunities are never lost, but someone will take the ones you miss."

"People don't injure their eyesight by looking at the bright side of things!"

If you are in a leadership position at work, remember that successful leaders…

- Understand the values of him/her and other teams, which in turn brings compassion to the workplace.
- Changes his/her perspective which creates more allowances for each other.
- Creates a feeling of consensus, thus binding the organisation together in remarkable ways.
- Practice living from the good values in the workplace, which in turn brings out the best in your team at all times.

Family

I am pretty much going to spend the most part sharing lessons which each of us can practise and learn within our family environment. My focus is on the children. The reason being that they have not yet been influenced by the media and society as much as the adults. If you want to see passion in action, look at a six year old child. Everything that is new they tackle with excitement. If you have your own children, you will relate immediately to my next point. Have you ever told your child that you are taking them to a theme park over the weekend? The days preceding the visit, what happens? The child asks every day how many sleeps still to go. They bounce up and down and get so excited. Same applies to the days before Christmas. Children show their excitement. Do you?

Basically, I want you to rediscover your passion through children. After all it's those small daily happenings that make life so spectacular. And when you have children - there are many such happenings. They can teach us many things.

Firstly, everyone you meet deserves to be greeted with a smile. Secondly, you should never say "no" to a gift from a child.

But let me backtrack a little, why is it that this excitement and passion disappears in children? I would like to answer this with a question. Do you remember when you were naughty as a child? What did your parents say to you? How did they scold you?

I bet it was something like this... "Wait until you grow up one day and become an adult, then you will see how tough life really is!"

Does this ring a bell? How many times did you hear it? Even worse, how many times have you said it to your own children? By saying stuff like this you are breaking down a child's passion for life. What do they have to look forward to in adulthood if all they hear how terrible it is. And then we wonder why the youth is so weird today!

Keep that magic going for as long as possible. Take a simple thing like believing in Father Christmas. I know people who told their children right from the word go that there is no such thing. This saddens me immensely – how do those children experience Christmas? The childhood fantasy land is where we build our creative thinking and visualisation – it's the stuff that makes us dream when we are adults. At the time of writing this book my daughters are eleven and thirteen. Peer pressure has now made them realise that there is no Santa Clause. But, this is how I explained it to them.

I told my girls that although the Santa one sees in films and on cartoons at the north pole may not be real – the 'spirit' of Christmas is. Each one of us can be Santa. Me, your mom, your aunt, your grandmother. It's by all of these people doing nice things and buying you gifts because they love you - in this way they carry on the Christmas spirit. Right now, I am Santa. One day when you are older, you will in turn do this for others.

At first, part of being Santa was keeping the illusion alive for younger siblings. I got to stay up late and wrap presents and fill the stocking. It meant drinking the milk and eating the cookies left for Santa. As I grew older, the Santa spirit grew. At university, my dorm mates and I played Secret Santas, delivering little gifts to each other during finals week.

Later in life, I'd drop off Christmas cookies to the nearest fire or police station on Christmas Eve. You can be Santa while shopping – whistling Christmas carols, wear bells that jingle, smile at those you pass – be patient with clerks. I hope my Santa spirit will be with me throughout the year, and that others will find the same joy that comes from being Santa Claus.

My girls are completely happy with that. Although my youngest definitely still believes in fairies. Why should I stop her – she's the most creative person in the family. Taking away fantasy makes humans hard and cold. Just look around you at those people that have a passion for life. They are dreamers, they have fun.

A few years ago I came home from a road show which I was emceeing and speaking at. My wife had been with the girls for over two weeks and wanted a break. As I walked into the door she gave me a shopping list and told me to take the girls with – she needed a break. What about me? Nevertheless, off I went, girls in hand. The shopping mall we were in happened to have some face painters strutting their stuff. Naturally my two girls loved this and pleaded to have their faces painted too! The more I resisted, the more they pleaded, bouncing up and down and not stopping.

To keep the peace, I gave in. Well, as soon as their faces were painted, they beamed. Everyone we walked past they smiled at and made sure people saw their colourful faces. They had fun. They laughed and made others laugh. They made me glad I had given in. That night back at home in the bath, they didn't want to wash off the paints.

Here now, my question to you. "Would you have your face painted in a shopping mall?" I guess not! I mean, what will the other shoppers think? What if someone you know sees you? Won't they think you've gone nuts?
What a silly notion to even suggest such an idea!

Are those your reactions? I assume they are. Last year at a conference I mentioned this story and as it turned out, two months later I bump into two ladies that had attended my talk. They came rushing up to me giggling, saying that they had taken my advice and actually had their faces painted. They just wanted to thank me, because that had been the best day of their lives. They laughed, joked and spoke to so many people – it was refreshing. In fact the same evening they visited a friend in hospital, and the medical staff didn't want them to leave, as they were cheering up everyone.

These two women had learnt a fantastic lesson. Let loose once in a while and discover your passion again. Don't be afraid of what others think. You are not hurting anyone, or doing any harm. You are merely having fun. We just don't play enough as adults.

On that note, let us talk about play. That's something we stopped doing as teenagers. Play as an adult is cuddling with your spouse and maybe tickling each other. But unfortunately that also doesn't last very long. Usually only the courting phase. (I suggest you read my book, 'The Art of Romance', if that's the case.)

However, we NEED to play as adults. A barbecue and getting sloshed doesn't count! Being silly and visiting a theme park is a start. But, in reality, the only adult play there is, is sex! That's the only time you get to fantasise, be creative and playful. So stop doing it under the sheets with the lights off! Learn to communicate and have fun. Many sex therapists say you should laugh during sex... after all, it's funny!

Bottom line, stop working nine to five, being stressed and moaning about life. Take time to 'play' and enjoy your life. That's the only way the passion is going to come back.

If you have fun and your children see you as a loving, touchy couple that still looks in each others eyes and laugh together, don't you think you are laying the foundation for your child to became a similar adult when they grow up?

By laying the correct foundations for your children now, you are ensuring that there will be a magical future world for our youth.

Finally, I want to share a few tips about finding love again. After all, what's the point of saying that we have to practise unconditional love and follow our heart in life when one doesn't know where to start searching for love.

Besides being honest with yourself and looking within, once again children can teach us many lessons about what love truly is. Their definitions are so simple, yet so to the point. Some should bring a tear to your heart and make you realise just how much love there is to give.

Here is what youngsters have to say when asked how they define love:

"Love is that first feeling you feel before all the bad stuff gets in the way."

Isn't that so true! Think about the first time you met your partner... it was infatuation. Everything was beautiful. You only saw the positive. Hence that saying, 'Love is blind.' Similarly, the first day you got that new job. In the beginning it was a challenge and adventure all in one. Now that you are used to it, it has become a rut? Therefore, if you have lost that initial 'infatuation' feeling, think back of that time and how it felt - this can bring the love feeling back again.

"When my grandmother got arthritis, she couldn't bend over and paint her toenails anymore. So my grandfather does it for her all the time, even when his hands got arthritis too. That's love."

Whatever you do in life, do you do it unselfishly? Do you carry on and try, even when it becomes difficult for you? When you love something, or someone purely, then this is exactly how you will behave.

"When someone loves you, the way they say your name is different. You know that your name is safe in their mouth."

Wow! This is so powerful. Think about your customers and clients. Do they feel comfortable and safe in their dealings with you? Do you radiate a confidence and passion for what you do that attracts them to your business? Do they spread the word about you by word of mouth? Do you find they enjoy spending time in your presence and buy from you rather than your company? If you can answer 'Yes' to these questions, only then can you confidently know that your passion is coming through to your customers.

"Love is when a girl puts on perfume and a boy puts on shaving cologne and they go out and smell each other."

I just had to throw this one in, it's cute. On a deeper level though, do you, and do your customers enjoy spending time with you? Do they feed off your knowledge and passion? Think about it!

"Love is when you go out to eat and give somebody most of your french fries without making them give you any of theirs," or "Love is when mommy gives daddy the best piece of chicken."

This is exactly what true love and passion is about. Do you do what you do in life unconditionally without expecting anything back in return. There is the story of a builder who was close to retirement. His boss asked him to build one last house. As he was near retirement, he didn't really feel like the task and did a rush job, cutting corners, using sub-standard items. Eventually when he completed the house, his boss turned around and gave him a set of keys saying, "Here are the keys to your house, it is a retirement present for all the great work you gave us during your career."

Sad if you think about it, the builder ended up living in his own sub-standard house. No-one was to blame, but himself. If you are truly passionate, you will always give 100% every time!

"Love is what makes you smile when you're tired."

How true is this? It doesn't matter what you do, there are always parts of your job which are not fun. Myself included. Examples are admin, VAT returns, etc. These are those tedious things we always try and put off. However, when you love what you do, these things become manageable, and because you are passionate about life and your career, it makes these things so much easier to cope with.

Believe it or not, you even manage to smile while doing the tax returns, because you know you had fun earning that money. Just imagine for one minute you hated your job and everything about it, and still have to do taxes? Which option would you go for?

On that note, I trust I have helped you light the fire within yourself so that your passion in what you do brings you the success you deserve in your life.

PROFESSIONAL SPEAKERS ASSOCIATION OF SOUTHERN AFRICA

PROFESSIONAL
S P E A K E R S
ASSOCIATION
OF SOUTHERN AFRICA

As the leading representative association for the speaking industry, we offer our members an active marketing platform, continued education and international networking in order to maximise turnover and quality.

Furthermore, as part of the Global Speakers Federation all PSASA members benefit of an international network of 6,000 experts globally.

Benefits of PSASA membership include:

1.) MORE **Quality** through regular events, knowledge sharing and international recognised certification.

2.) Opportunity to obtain **Certified Speaking Professional (CSP)** Accreditation.

3.) MORE **Turnover** as a direct result of meeting national and international experts and related industry partners such as meeting planners, bureaus, etc.

4.) MORE **Innovation** as a result of a global benchmark.

5.) MORE **Exposure** to the market through the PSASA website, our member directory, events and search engine optimisation.

6.) MORE **Transparency** through MORE Fun in what you do, because of the unique spirit of who we are.

Visit our website for full details:
www.psasouthernafrica.co.za